Wrestling with the Divine

THEOLOGY AND THE SCIENCES
Kevin J. Sharpe, Series Editor

BOARD OF ADVISORS

TITLES IN THE SERIES

Wrestling *with the* *Divine*

Religion, Science, and Revelation

Christopher C. Knight

FORTRESS PRESS

MINNEAPOLIS

WRESTLING WITH THE DIVINE
Religion, Science, and Revelation

Scripture is from The New English Bible, copyright © 1961, 1970 by the Delegates of the Oxford University Press and the Syndics of the Cambridge University Press. Reprinted by permission.

Cover art: Wassily Kandinsky, *Deluge.* © 2001 Superstock, Inc. Used by permission.
Cover design: David Meyer
Book design: Michelle L. Norstad

Library of Congress Cataloging-in-Publication Data
Knight, Christopher C.
    Wrestling with the divine : religion, science, and Revelation / Christopher C. Knight.
        p. cm. — (Theology and the sciences series)
    Includes bibliographical references and index.
    ISBN 0-8006-3298-2 (alk. paper)
  1. Revelation. I. Title. II. Theology and the sciences.

BT127.2 .K64 2001
231.7'4—dc21   2001025853

The paper used in this publication meets the minimum requirements for American National Standard for Information Sciences—Permanence of Paper for Printed Library Materials, ANSI Z329.48–1984.

Manufactured in the U.S.A.   AF 1-3298

This book is dedicated

to my children

Elspeth

Catriona

Iona

and

Rupert

Contents

Preface

Many people still think that scientific knowledge necessarily undermines religious faith. Those who hold such faith in scorn are, therefore, often surprised when they discover that many professional scientists are also religious believers. Can it be possible, they ask, that the psychological hold of religious belief is so strong that even scientists can become irrational when in its grip?

Sadly, the existence of scientists who are also religious fundamentalists provides at least some evidence that this can be the case. By questioning well-established scientific theory, simply because it clashes with a literalist reading of the scriptures of their faith, such people enter a world of convoluted rationality that would smack of intellectual dishonesty if not for the evident passion with which they pursue their goal.

The position of the vast majority of believing scientists is, however, quite different from this fundamentalist one. Far from feeling the need to question well-established scientific theory, they believe that there is nothing in such theory that is incompatible with their faith. They have learned from theologians to understand religious language in terms both of the culture within which a particular revelation has been received and of the specifically religious meaning of that revelation.

Thus, for example, when most believing scientists read the creation narratives in Genesis, they do not see them as quasi-scientific accounts of the process by which the cosmos came to be. Rather, they accept the theologians' understanding of them as essentially poetical accounts of the purposes of God in the cosmos, expressed in prescientific terms because of the culture within which they were received and developed. They do not see those narratives as contradicting the scientific account of the mechanisms through which the cosmos evolved to its present degree of complexity, but rather as pointing to God as the originator and upholder of those mechanisms.

By listening to theologians and to their interpreters, most believing scientists have, in this way, been able to see the fundamentalist agenda not only as scientifically futile but also as theologically unnecessary. They have not, however, been simply passive receivers of the current theological consensus. Some of the more thoughtful of them have, in fact, gone on to disagree with many of the theologians who up to this point have been their guides. Instead of simply accepting the common theological assertion that scientific and religious languages always refer to different realms of human experience—and that therefore any question of how they interact is a meaningless one—these scientists have suggested that a division between mechanism and meaning, though useful as an indication of the primary purposes of scientific and religious languages, should not be taken as axiomatic. For, they say, their scientific knowledge has in practice sometimes enlarged and clarified their understanding of God's purposes and actions—an understanding they received through the religious language of their faith. In this sense at least, the two languages are not independent of one another.

Moreover, they point out, this enlargement and clarification of theological understanding has often had the effect of making that understanding more credible than when expressed solely in traditional terms. Thus, they suggest, a "dialogue of science and theology" is not only important as a fruitful strand of intellectual endeavor; it should also be seen as an important apologetic weapon, especially in a culture that assumes the incompatibility of scientific understanding and religious belief.

The original stimulus for my own exploration of the relationship between science and theology was, in fact, the literature that has expressed this view. Inspired by the work of pioneers like Arthur Peacocke and John Polkinghorne (the former an Oxford biochemist, the latter a Cambridge physicist), I thought that my academic background in both theology and astrophysics might enable me to play a part in the dialogue that they had fostered. When an opportunity for study and teaching on this subject within the University of Cambridge came my way, I grasped it eagerly. It was exhilarating to think that I might be able not only to contribute to the growth of theological understanding, but also to reassure a confused generation that traditional Christian beliefs are compatible with serious scientific commitment and knowledge.

Within a year or two of beginning systematic study of the issues, however, I found myself—rather to my consternation— becoming increasingly critical of at least some of the existing literature. Indeed, the more I explored the coherence of certain types of argument that had become widely accepted, the more I found myself drawn to different and less orthodox conclusions—ones with which many religious believers would, I knew, be less than happy.

These insights emerged mainly from two strands of the dialogue between science and theology as it then stood. One of these strands attempted to deal with the question of how we can talk coherently about the way God acts in the world. The prime question that arose for me from this discussion of divine action was one that, as we shall see, Peacocke had already broached—how the mode or modes of such action should be related to the nature of revelatory experience. I soon came to believe that this could best be done in terms of human psychology. I was encouraged by the knowledge that others, from a quite different perspective, had also thought of such experience in psychological terms. The other strand of the dialogue of science and theology that became central to my thinking was that which had attempted to explore the relationship between scientific and religious language usage. Both of these lines of exploration, it seemed to me, led naturally to a number of questions that had, despite their topicality in the wider theological community, been treated only very inadequately by those involved in the dialogue of science and theology.

Could it be, I wondered, that because so many of those involved in that dialogue had developed their arguments in an apologetic context, they were blind to implications of their own arguments that might subvert the defense of the faith to which they were committed? This suspicion prompted me to attempt to separate what seemed theologically fruitful in their work from what was essentially apologetic. Somewhat to my surprise, this resulted not only in a radical undermining of the cozy Christian orthodoxy of at least one strand of modern writing about science and religion, but also in the emergence of a fruitful perspective on many theological issues.

Among these issues were not only many that had long been central to the science and religion debate but also some that the debate had tended to ignore. In particular, it seemed to me that my new perspective had important ramifications for developing the sort of theology of the world's faiths for which many were striving.

I went on to outline some components of this synthesis in articles published in academic journals.[1] The restricted length of such articles meant, however, that their wider theological implications, which to me constituted their prime interest, could only be hinted at. Something considerably longer than a journal article was clearly necessary; it was with this in mind that I set out to write what eventually became this book. My intention was to explore the relationship of the ideas outlined in the articles to one another, to the wider dialogue of science and theology, and, indeed, to the entire theological enterprise as it enters the twenty-first century.

It became apparent to me soon after I began this task, however, that a choice lay before me. One possibility was to embark straightaway on an exhaustive exploration of these relationships. This, I judged, would require a book (or even a series of books) much lengthier and more complex than anyone but the specialist theologian or philosopher of religion would attempt to read. Alternatively I could, initially at least, attempt an essay that, by virtue of its brevity, would be accessible to a wide audience. Rightly or wrongly, I have chosen the latter option, with all its attendant risks. While I recognize that a much fuller presentation of my arguments will become necessary—especially because philosophical theology spills over in my thinking into systematic theology—it seems appropriate at this stage of my work to present something rather less ambitious. *Wrestling with the Divine* is essentially an introduction to a more detailed study—long enough to indicate clearly my general thesis, but concise enough for that thesis not to be obscured by a wealth of detail and cross-reference.

It is for the reader to judge whether I have succeeded in striking this balance. The attempt to do so, at any rate, explains why I have made no attempt to survey the entire science and religion debate of recent years. Although I refer to a number of authors in the field, these have been chosen to illustrate particular aspects of my argument rather than to provide a textbook account of the current state of debate. Similarly, when discussing issues that lie outside the mainstream of that debate, I have concentrated on a few significant theologians in each area, using their work as a springboard for those who wish to follow up these aspects of my argument in a more systematic manner. For much the same reason I have kept footnotes to a minimum.

I have also decided to avoid, wherever possible, discussion of issues that require an explanation of scientific technicalities. In my teaching experience, nonscientists react to such technicalities either by getting bogged down in essentially peripheral matters or else by running a mile. This tendency—as I note in the first section of the essay—has had an extremely detrimental effect on the whole science and religion debate, and my main purpose in writing this essay is to put certain questions emerging from that debate firmly on the theological and philosophical agenda. The reader who is fond of what has sometimes been called the "gee whiz" approach to the popularization of science may, as a result, be somewhat disappointed by what follows. Those with little or no background or interest in the sciences, on the other hand, may find it comforting to be assured at this stage that, though reference to scientific technicalities has very occasionally proved unavoidable in what follows, it is firmly on theological and philosophical issues that I shall be concentrating.

Finally, some have held that much of the current interest in the science and religion debate is based on a "spectatorial empiricism" imported from the sciences. A critic of this sort might, therefore, like to know that the theological reflection that has given rise to this essay has brought me—over a period of years—to a position far less conservative than that from which I started. This journey has been a reluctant and not untroubled one. At times, I have felt less like a scientific spectator than like Jacob of the Genesis story, struggling with the angel. This inner conflict—which still goes on—has, I hope, had no influence on the coherence of my arguments. Here and there, nevertheless, the perceptive reader may find evidence that the formulation of my arguments has involved not only the intellectual equivalent of toil and sweat, but also the spiritual equivalent of blood and tears.

This essay reflects my conviction that theological formulation, like every other aspect of the spiritual life, necessarily involves something that pertains to the whole human person, and not just to the rational faculty as understood by Enlightenment thinkers. The Greek fathers referred to this sometimes in terms of the "heart" (*kardia*) and sometimes in terms of the "intellect" (*nous*); it is eloquent of the impoverishment of our spiritual vocabulary that no current translation of those terms indicates to us anything other than the seat of sentiment or of logic. The deeper, integrating, contemplative faculty to which the terms originally referred is, sadly, something about which we can no longer speak straightforwardly. It remains, nevertheless, the source of all true theology.

1

Science and Theology in Dialogue

For many years, there has been a significant gap between the concerns and perspectives of the ordinary, intelligent Christian and those of the academic theologian. This gap has, it must be admitted, been due in part to the timidity of preachers and others with a duty to build bridges across it. It has also, however, had a more natural cause: that of simple delayed reaction. The professional theologian has, understandably, usually been a year or two (if not a generation or two) ahead of the typical person in the pew.

In one area, however—that of the relationship between science and theology—the time lag between the professional theologian and the intelligent layperson has often been the other way around. Here, fascinatingly, it has often been the religiously inclined professional scientist who is running ahead, while the professional theologian is slow to respond.

This tardiness has not, it would seem, been due to any lack of appreciation of the impact of the sciences on modern thinking. Keith Ward, for example, speaks for the vast majority of his theological colleagues when he notes that there have essentially been three great movements of thought that have brought about a revision of traditional religious attitudes: "the rise of the natural sciences, the growth of historical understanding and the acceptance of critical thinking."[1] While the insights of the last two have long been part of the toolbox of the modern theologian, insights arising from an informed knowledge of the natural sciences have had relatively little part to play in mainstream theological enterprise.

A number of factors have played their part in this. One has undoubtedly been the recognition that the scientific expertise on which such work must be built is notoriously difficult to obtain for those who have not had standard training. Most theologians have had no such training and are therefore understandably wary of falling into oversimplification or downright error in scientific matters. They do not forget the kind of trap into which Hugh Montefiore once fell, when he claimed that there was no obvious neo-Darwinian reason for the whiteness of polar bears. (They had no predators to treat them as prey, he reasoned, so why should they need camouflage?) This statement was, understandably, gleefully pounced on by biologist and arch-atheist Richard Dawkins, who not only pointed out Montefiore's failure to understand that camouflage is as important for predators as for prey, but also lampooned his presumption in making such a statement. Montefiore should, said Dawkins, strictly have written: "I personally, off the top of my head sitting in my study, never having visited the Arctic, never having seen a polar bear in the wild, and having been educated in classical literature and theology, have not so far managed to think of a reason why polar bears might benefit from being white."[2]

If at least some theologians do not forget this sort of problem, however, what many of them do seem to forget (or to ignore) is that a genuine dialogue[3] of science and theology can best take place when scientists and theologians, each with their own expertise, are able to engage in conversation based on each others' questions, each refining the others' perspectives in what a scientist might call an iterative cycle. This does not require that theologians have any particular scientific insight, but it does require a degree of teamwork that, to most members of the theological community, seems uncongenial. Why this might be so is unclear. What is observable is that while scientific books and papers frequently have several authors, theological ones only rarely do. The result of this tendency is that the modern dialogue of science and theology has only infrequently involved a dialogue of scientists and theologians. It has largely continued as it began: as a dialogue within the minds of particular individuals of scientific background who have attempted to combine their expert scientific knowledge with their sometimes less-than-expert theological perspectives.

The lack of theological expertise—among at least some of the scientists interested in the possibility of a dialogue of science and theology—has been exacerbated by the fact that their work has often arisen not from specifically theological concerns, but from apologetic ones. If we look at the literature on the subject over the last quarter of the twentieth century, we find that a significant proportion of it has come from the pens of what we might call "scientist-apologists"[4]: people who are—or at least were when they began their task—working scientists rather than theologians.

Even major figures in the dialogue, such as Arthur Peacocke and John Polkinghorne, fall into this category, since the perceived need to make Christian believing credible in a scientific age clearly provided not only their initial motivation for working on that dialogue, but also the framework that led them, in the earlier stages of their work, to tackle particular questions in particular ways. As a result, their growing theological expertise was often impressive but one-sided, gained at the prompting of the needs of the dialogue as they saw it at a particular time rather than reflecting a full awareness of the issues that were important to other theologians.

The resulting failure of many theologians to take the dialogue of science and theology seriously was made worse by the way some of the scientist-apologists' theological perspectives were at times distinctly reminiscent of the sort of "natural theology" that had arisen, largely under the impetus of the rise of modern science, in the middle of the seventeenth century. Polkinghorne, for example, has consistently called quite explicitly for the development of a "revived and revised natural theology" based at least in part on the way science "seems to throw up questions which point beyond itself and transcend its power to answer. They arise from recognizing the potentiality inherent in the structure of the world, its interlocking tightly-knit character, and, indeed, its very intelligibility which makes it open to our own inquiry."[5]

This appeal to the tradition of natural theology has only rarely, however, been greeted with even lukewarm enthusiasm by professional theologians. If the medieval tradition of natural theology, with its appeal to purely philosophical arguments, has never quite lost its fascination for some of them, it is widely held in their community that the sort of natural theology that appeals to the nature of the cosmos should be treated with the gravest suspicion. Nicholas Lash, for example, undoubtedly speaks for the vast majority of his theological colleagues when he fulminates against "the fatuous illusion that we could discover or come across God as a fact about the world."[6]

Even in his earlier work, Polkinghorne, it must be said, was not unaware of this antipathy. The approach he then advocated was, he

recognized, one that was "undergoing a welcome revival in our time
. . . not so much at the hands of the theologians . . . but at the hands
of the scientists."[7] He attributed this, however, largely to the historical failure of a particular form of natural theology in the face of
Darwin's insights into evolution through chance processes.

In this Polkinghorne was undoubtedly partially right. For rather
than simply signifying the study of theology in terms of philosophical logic or of knowledge of the natural world, the term natural theology has often been associated with a particular version of it that
developed in the latter part of the seventeenth century, only to be
discredited by scientific advances some two centuries later. The term
was associated during that period largely with quasi-scientific arguments for the existence of God—in particular that which pointed to
the world's complexity and interrelatedness as a sure indication of
its design by an intelligent and benevolent creator. Until the acceptance of evolutionary theory in the wake of Darwin's *The Origin of
Species,* such an argument was, indeed, often the mainstay of religious apologetic.[8] Darwin's insights into the evolution of the natural
order from simplicity to complexity through natural processes, however, rightly consigned such arguments to the waste heap of intellectual history. Once it had been recognized that a theological view of
the natural world could use design arguments only with the greatest
caution and with numerous qualifications,[9] the whole enterprise of
natural theology—which in that period had such arguments at its
heart—came to be viewed with the greatest suspicion.

A second reason for treating natural theology with suspicion
arose, however, from a quite different cause, which Polkinghorne
seems to have recognized fully only in his more recent work. This
was that natural theology had often been associated with a neglect of
the concept of revelation in a way that seemed to many to be a dilu-
tion of Christian theology. Whereas the seventeenth-century proponents of arguments from design had often seen them as providing a
complement to the theology of "revealed religion," the next century
had witnessed, in deism, a development of natural theology that
tended to bypass specific revelations of God. In this deistic appropriation of natural theology, it was assumed that there existed a "reasonable and universal religious faith" that was evident from the
creation itself, independent of any specific revelation. Such a faith, it
was held, consisted simply of belief in a Supreme Being, in the
immortality of the soul, and in the obligation to moral conduct.

Matthew Tindal's *Christianity as Old as Creation* (1730), for example, held the Christian Bible to represent not a unique revelation but a republication of these three essential tenets.

Moreover, even when revelation was not effectively ignored in this way, there was still a tendency (as there had been in its medieval manifestations) for natural theology to be developed independently of special revelation. It was, as Thomas Torrance has rightly noted, "pursued as an independent conceptual system, claiming to have its value precisely in that independent status, as a sort of *praeambula fidei*, antecedent to positive theology, fulfilling a mediating and apologetic function."[10]

In the earlier part of the present century, this particular suspicion of natural theology was reinforced among many Protestants by the work of Karl Barth. Reacting strongly against much of the religious philosophy of his time, with its positive attitude to science, culture, and religious experience, Barth sought to call Christians back to what he saw as the Reformation reliance on God's sole revelation in Jesus Christ. All natural theology or theology rooted in religious experience was, he held, radically and inevitably perverted by the depravity of all human capacities since "the Fall." If Barth himself shifted his position on the subject of natural theology somewhat as he got older,[11] there can be no doubt that a diluted version of what was taken to be the "Barthian" view became, and remains, widely influential.

This influence has not been without its good effects. In particular, the approaches of people like Thomas Torrance, clearly inspired in part by Barth's later work, have pointed to the need for great methodological caution when insights from the world of science are used to enlarge and clarify the traditional doctrinal framework that has arisen from the Christian revelation. The way Torrance has used insights from Albert Einstein's physics to explore the concept of incarnation in relation to space and time,[12] for example, has not only contributed much to the elucidation of that doctrine, but has done so in a way that demonstrates a clear (if arguably too narrow) view of the nature of revelation. Not only does Torrance hold that the doctrine of the incarnation, as an expression of God's revelation of himself in Christ, will be revisable only within strict limits; he also attempts to justify those limits in a way that is theologically articulate.

In his more recent work in particular, Torrance has developed a view that holds that while insights from the natural sciences can properly be used in our expression of what God has revealed, the link between the resulting natural theology and the "positive theology" that arises from revelation must remain unbroken. Seeing this link as analogous to that between geometry and physics, he uses as an example the way Euclidean geometry was, as a prior conceptual system, ultimately found to be irrelevant to the actual structure of the world as perceived in Einstein's general theory of relativity. Similarly, he claims, any a priori natural theology will fail to be adequate to the actual reality of God's revelatory action in the world. Thus, he claims, a proper natural theology "cannot be pursued in its traditional abstractive form, as a prior conceptual system on its own, but must be brought within the body of positive theology and be pursued in indissoluble unity with it. . . . It will function as the necessary intrastructure of theological science, in which we are concerned to unfold and express the rational forms of understanding that arise under the compulsion of the intelligible reality of God's self-revelation."[13]

In Torrance's own work, however, the necessary link between revelation and the nature of the cosmos is affirmed largely in terms of what he sees as the necessity of rejecting "a deistic disjunction between God and the world"[14]—a "dualism" that in his view links the two main eras of speculation in natural theology, that beginning with the scholasticism of the twelfth century and that beginning with the work of religious scientists in the seventeenth.[15] When we look closely at how Torrance uses the word *dualism*, however, we find that it is linked to a way of talking about revelation and Divine Providence that in fact manifests another sort of dualism: that which, like much Barthian theology, separates the transcendence and the immanence of God—his "otherness" and his presence in his creation—to such an extent that the latter is effectively ignored and is certainly devalued. In discussing the main traditions of natural theology, for example, Torrance speaks of them as rooted in an approach that "attempts to reach and teach knowledge of God *apart altogether* from *any* interaction between God and the world" (emphasis added).[16] While such words may represent a slip of the pen and certainly need to be understood in the context of Torrance's entire argument, they seem to be eloquent of the fundamental Barthian stance in which that argument is rooted. Providential interaction between God and the world, that stance suggests, is something quite different—"apart altogether"—from the general interaction that occurs in the processes of the natural world.

Moreover, however we judge issues such as these, Torrance's view is still essentially rooted in a view of Christian uniqueness that is intrinsic to the Barthian framework. The sort of consideration that has emerged in relation to interfaith dialogue in recent years simply has no place in his scheme of things. The "intelligible reality of God's self-revelation" of which he speaks is identified with *Christian* revelation. His arguments for the necessity of the gift of revelation for real theological knowledge give rise to, or are set within, a framework in which, arbitrarily, only certain revelatory experiences are taken as definitive. While, as we shall see, there may be grounds for arguing for an account of the Christian revelation that allows it this character, a neo-Barthian account such as Torrance's fails to examine these grounds.

Despite these drawbacks, however, Torrance's approach not only remains the most exhaustive and potentially fruitful account of the relationship of a scientifically informed theology of nature to revelation that has appeared thus far, but also highlights the lack of such an examination in much of the current dialogue of science and theology. In the earlier work of Peacocke and Polkinghorne, in particular, the epistemological questions highlighted by Torrance were largely unacknowledged. While their approach did not manifest a deistic disregard for revelation, it simply bypassed important questions about the nature and content of revelation.[17] By contrast, at the heart of much that follows is a recognition that the theological concept of revelation is a key one, not only for understanding what has been fruitful in the dialogue of science and theology as it has emerged from the insights of the scientist-apologists, but also for developing it further.

This recognition arises in part from the more recent work of Polkinghorne, in which his earlier and perhaps somewhat simplistic call for a revised natural theology has been expanded in an attempt to articulate more fully the way theology should respond to insights from the natural sciences. For while he is happy to join the many who would now argue that science and religion "have important things to say to each other,"[18] he is less than happy with some of the things that others believe are actually being said. It is, he argues, vital that the broader understanding of Christian doctrine, which inevitably accompanies any interaction of science and theology, is developed with a proper regard for both the scope and limits of that interaction. Otherwise, he seems to fear, illegitimate developments of Christian theology may become widely accepted because of a supposed scientific basis.

In this respect, he suggests, the many approaches that assume a proper interaction of science and theology should be classified not, as is usually done in the wake of Ian Barbour's work,[19] into those of "dialogue" and those of "integration," but instead, in terms of "consonance" and "assimilation." The term *consonance* should be used, says Polkinghorne, to indicate those approaches, like his own, in which science "does not determine theological thought but . . . constrains it. . . . The scientific and theological accounts of the world must fit together in a mutually consistent way."[20] More radical approaches, he suggests, involve "assimilation" in the sense of attempting "a degree of accommodation of the one to the other that could seem to threaten [theology's] justified autonomy."[21] (Here, of course, we have something comparable to Torrance's insistence on the controlling character of "positive theology," and Torrance does indeed seem to be one of the influences on Polkinghorne's later work.)

While asserting theology's autonomy, however, Polkinghorne does not make any real analysis of it. His attitude is indicated, nevertheless, by the fact that he finds threats to it in the work of both Ian Barbour and Arthur Peacocke who, far from denying the autonomy of theology, actually stress it. Peacocke, for example, is insistent that "the concepts and theories theologians develop . . . should not be prematurely reduced, without adequate proof, to the concepts and theories of other disciplines appropriate to man, society and nature."[22] What Polkinghorne regards as his "assimilation" is not, therefore, based on any theoretical disregard for the autonomy of theology. Rather, as becomes clear from Polkinghorne's subsequent discussion, the charge of assimilation is to be attached to any willingness to allow scientific insights to suggest an interpretation of Christian doctrines that might be considered unorthodox. What Polkinghorne actually means by assimilation seems, in fact, to have less to do with theological autonomy as such than with assumptions about the boundaries of legitimate doctrinal change.

Implicit assumptions of this sort are, of course, to be found in the work of all theologians. Where the work of Peacocke and Polkinghorne differs from that of most others, however, is that the coherence of their respective judgments on this issue is susceptible to a critique based upon a theme that is central to both their approaches.

For both, right from the beginning of their theological work, have manifested a stress on the immanence of God in creation, intimately linked to their understandings of the way he may be said to act in the world. This emphasis has, as we shall see in the next chapter, provided persuasive solutions to some of the problems associated with the concept of divine action. While Polkinghorne has used it largely to defend the Christian revelation as traditionally understood, however, Peacocke has used it to explore fascinating new possibilities. These possibilities, I shall argue, not only constitute the more coherent approach of the two, but also may be developed further in a way that is extremely fruitful.

2

Divine Action
and Pansacramental Naturalism

In a recent sermon, Arthur Peacocke retold, in quasi-biblical terms, "the story of how the very material stuff of the world became *persons*—of how matter-energy in space-time had the inherent capacity to become free, self-conscious persons who can know each other— and have the spiritual capacity to know God, if they so choose."[1] His "Genesis for the Third Millennium" went as follows:

> There was God. And God was All-That-Was. God's Love overflowed and God said: "Let Other be. And let there be Laws for what it is and what it can be—and let it explore its possibilities and potentialities." And there was Other, a field of energy, which exploded as the Universe from a point ten or so billion years in our time. Swirling basic matter appeared, expanded and expanded and cooled into clouds of gas, bathed in radiant light. Still the Universe went on expanding and condensing into swirling whirlpools of matter and light—a billion galaxies. Five billion years ago, one star in one galaxy—our Sun—attracted around it matter as planets. One of them was our Earth. There the assembly of atoms and the temperature became just right to allow some molecules to become large and complex enough to make copies of themselves—the first specks of life. Life multiplied and burst into many forms. Mammals appeared and began to develop complex brains, which enabled them to learn. Among these were creatures who lived in trees. From these our first ancestors derived and then, only forty thousand years or so ago, the first men and women appeared. They began to know about themselves and what they were doing—they were not only conscious but also self-conscious. The

first word, the first laugh were heard. The first paintings were made. The first sense of destiny beyond—with the first signs of hope, for they buried their dead with ritual. The first prayers were made to the One who made All-That-Is and All-That-Is-becoming. The first experiences of goodness, beauty and truth—but also of their opposites—human beings had free will.[2]

A central feature of the story is summed up in the phrase "Let Other be. And let there be Laws for what it is and what it can be—and let it explore its possibilities and potentialities." The rest of the story is then told without direct reference to God until he emerges as part of the consciousness of human beings. Intrinsic to this account of the creation is the idea that once the cosmos had emerged from the big bang, no action of God, over and above sustaining it in being, was necessary for the emergence of life or of consciousness within it. Those qualities are, rather, assumed to be inherent, divinely willed potentialities of that Other that has its origin and sustenance in the overflowing of God's love.

In Peacocke's more formal work, both the scientific and the theological justification for this perspective are argued at length. Certain aspects of this argument are peculiar to his own way of thinking. Much of it, however, is related to a now common emphasis on the immanence of God in creation, which has arisen from the widespread recognition that, from a modern scientific perspective, a coherent theological view of God's action in the world must involve recognition of the central role of natural processes.[3]

This stress—which has been a strong, almost a defining characteristic of the dialogue of science and theology in recent years—has arisen in part from a reaction against what has been called the "God of the gaps" approach to the relationship between God and the world. In this approach—still, alas, often seen in the popular mind as an intrinsic part of any theistic understanding—divine action is seen as located in those aspects of the world that cannot be explained in scientific terms. In very early versions of it, for example, lightning and floods were seen as supernatural divine acts. In later versions—by which time such "acts of God" had been seen as explicable in scientific terms—the "gaps" that appeared to require special divine intervention were such things as the emergence of life and consciousness in the cosmos.[4]

Not only had this approach been disastrous in apologetic terms, as one "gap" after another became susceptible to scientific analysis. In addition, as some began to realize, its basis in an understanding of God's occasional intervention in the natural order could be objected to on purely theological grounds as well. Aubrey Moore, for example, argued this point of view over a century ago, in relation to the way any interpretation of the Genesis accounts, in terms of the creation of the world in a series of supernatural acts, was undermined by Darwin's evolutionary theory. Darwin's understanding was, Moore argued, not only far from being inimical to a Christian understanding, but actually highly constructive. For, he suggested, insofar as it involves an understanding of God's creative activity, the Darwinian view is "infinitely more Christian than the theory of 'special creation.' For it implies the immanence of God in nature, and the omnipresence of His creative power." Indeed, he went on, those "who oppose the doctrine of evolution in defense of a 'continued intervention' of God, seem to have failed to notice that a theory of occasional intervention implies as its correlative a theory of ordinary absence."[5]

This "ordinary absence," it would seem, is what people like Peacocke and Polkinghorne have tried to counter in their emphasis on the immanence of God in creation, stressing that all natural processes should be seen as part of God's continuing action in the world. As Polkinghorne has affirmed, in a comparison of his work with that of Peacocke, both seek to talk of divine agency as "continuously at work in a way consistent with the known laws of nature (themselves understood theologically as expressions of God's faithful and unchanging will for his creation). [Both] refuse the word 'intervention' . . . as the way to speak about divine acts."[6]

An important aspect of this noninterventionist account of divine action, particularly in the work of Peacocke, has been a stress on the evolutionary creativity to be found in the interplay of chance and physical law.[7] As he has put it, "it has become increasingly apparent that it is chance operating within a lawlike framework that is the basis of the inherent creativity of the natural order, its ability to generate new forms, patterns and organizations of matter and energy. . . . To a theist, it is now clear that God creates in the world *through* what we call 'chance' operating within the created order, each stage of which constitutes the launching pad for the next."[8]

What "emerges" through the increasing complexity of the cosmos—life and consciousness for example—can thus be seen as both natural, from a scientific perspective, and in conformity with the divine purpose, from a theological one. (As Fraser Watts has observed, employing the analogy of the languages used to describe mental processes and to describe the underlying physical processes of the brain, a use of two levels of description for a single process is entirely legitimate and is a salutary reminder that theological description is not simply something that becomes appropriate when other types of description are unavailable.)[9]

This stress on divine action through natural processes has not, moreover, been limited to events or processes that can be understood straightforwardly in terms of natural emergence through increasing cosmic complexity. Polkinghorne has also suggested, for example, that "miracles"—the prime acts that have traditionally been thought of in supernatural terms—might also be thought of in terms other than those of divine intervention in the natural course of events. They might better, he suggests, be seen in terms analogous to changes of "regime" in the physical world, in which the same underlying physical laws give rise to sudden changes of physical behavior.[10] (To illustrate this he uses the phenomenon of superconductivity: the complete disappearance of electrical resistivity in certain materials below a certain threshold temperature. This provides a clear example of how discontinuous and at first, seemingly inexplicable changes in the cosmos can be the result of underlying continuities.)

The way that this type of approach appears to allow at least some of the purposes of God to be carried out without recourse to supernatural intervention has proved an attractive one to many. A question that naturally arises from it has, however, recently emerged as an important one within the science and theology debate: Which—if any—aspects of divine action need to be understood as involving God in ways over and above the inherent fruitfulness of the divinely willed and divinely sustained mass-energy content and natural laws of the cosmos? Does the tendency to see less and less of God's action as beyond analysis in terms of natural processes, it is asked, mean that we should now abandon all attempts to reserve certain areas of God's action as intrinsically beyond such analysis? Can we, in fact, now adopt a naturalism in which divine action and divinely willed natural processes are simply identified with one another?

Polkinghorne's response to this question seems to have been strongly influenced by the fear of "assimilation," which we have already noted. In particular, he has reacted strongly against any sort of Christology inspired by a general focus on divine action through evolutionary emergence, seeing grave dangers in Peacocke's view of Christ's incarnation as "an example of that emergence-from-continuity that characterizes the creative process."[11] Increasingly, in fact, Polkinghorne seems to have had to put a gloss on his previous writings in order to prevent what he sees as this sort of "assimilation" of theology to scientific understanding.[12] One of the focuses of his recent work in this respect has been on the concept of the personhood of God. This concept, he claims, requires a recognition of divine action over and above what he calls its "impersonal, relatively deistic mode." It is also necessary, in his view, to recognize examples of "Creatorly action in a more personal mode"; otherwise, he thinks, one will be guilty of "an implicit deism . . . whose nakedness is only thinly covered by a garment of personalized metaphor."[13]

He has explored this distinction largely in terms of a divine interference with the world that is "noninterventionist" only in the weak sense that it takes place without any setting aside of the laws of nature. He argues that the nondeterministic nature of the physical world as seen by the modern physicist allows for divine action to be hidden "within the inescapably cloudy unpredictabilities of physical process, interpreted . . . as the sites of ontological openness."[14]

Peacocke too, it must be said, has recently felt the need to make a similar distinction. Having talked so eloquently for many years about the divinely willed fruitfulness of natural processes, he has now begun to differentiate between God's providential and creative action, despite recognizing how "unhelpful" the "distinction between creation and providence often proves to be."[15] This has become necessary to him, it would seem, because of the assumption (which he shares with Polkinghorne) that because God's providential "response" to the world—to prayer, for example—occurs in a temporal universe, God himself must be seen as experiencing the events of that universe and responding to them in a temporal way.

This assumption, as Polkinghorne himself has noted,[16] seems to be in tension with other aspects of Peacocke's approach, which seem in many respects more consonant with the "single act" account of divine action in which the "acts" of God are understood in relation to "the classical view of divine eternity"[17] in which God's being is timeless. This latter view has not only had important modern proponents such as Austin Farrer,[18] but also has an impressive pedigree, going back at least as far as Thomas Aquinas, for whom "God is wholly outside the order of time, standing, as it were, in the high citadel of eternity, which is all at one time. The whole course of time is subject to eternity in one simple glance."[19]

Peacocke's susceptibility to the accounts of God's "involvement" by people like Jürgen Moltmann and W. H. Vanstone[20] has been such, however, that he has sought to reconcile a view of God's creative action through a single act, "Let Other be," with a view of the "providential" aspect of divine action that eschews a single act account. He seems to suggest that this is necessary to enable him to focus "upon *particular* events, or patterns of events, as expressive of the 'purposes' (e.g., of communication) of God, who is thereby conceived of as in some sense personal."[21] This aim is not, however, incompatible with a single act account, which must necessarily provide an explanation for particular events in terms of the divine purpose.[22] It is therefore somewhat surprising that Peacocke should at times try so hard to fit his belief in divine providence into a "separate acts" mold, especially because the single act account provides a way of avoiding, as he seems to wish, the dualism inherent in making a firm distinction between creative and providential acts.

Moreover, Peacocke's reluctance to embrace the single act model is all the more mystifying in that he is not in the position of being unable to see the simplistic nature of J. R. Lucas's assertion—with which Polkinghorne seems to agree—that to "deny the temporality of God is to deny that he is personal in any sense in which we understand personality."[23] Peacocke's work has included a persuasive attempt to explore how "the stuff of the world, the primeval concourse of protons, neutrinos, photons, etc. has, as a matter of fact and not conjecture, become persons—human beings who possess 'inner' self-conscious lives in relation to other human beings."[24] His reflections on personality in the light of this, which includes a defense of the propriety of talking about God's "supra-personal"[25] nature, certainly provides, at least implicitly, a broader view of the divine nature than that assumed by those who see it as precluding any sort of single act account of divine action.

The way Peacocke develops his temporal view of providential divine action is, it must be said, far from unsubtle, in that he sees the mode of such action in terms of the analogy of "whole-part constraint." This is the way that complex wholes can, in a scientific perspective, be seen as having an effect on the parts of which they are made up. When providential divine action is thought of in light of whole-part constraint, he suggests it can "be envisaged as able to exercise constraints upon events in the myriad sub-levels of existence that constitute that 'world' without abrogating the laws and regularities that specifically pertain to them—and this without 'intervening' in . . . unpredictabilities."[26]

The general question of God's relationship to time is, however, a complex one—both in terms of scientific argument[27] and of theological ramification[28]—and it is therefore fortunate that a judgment of the relative merits of this whole-part constraint scheme and a single act account of divine action is not definitive for my argument in the remainder of this essay. Peacocke's stress on God's providential action being always on the "world-as-a-whole"—while arguably incompatible with a response-within-time model for purely scientific reasons[29]—links such action in an important way to the creative mode of that action. In both cases, the desired "result" is seen as emerging through processes entirely intrinsic to the world, and not from interference with some part of it. This means that the distinction between the two modes of action is far less definitive than in Polkinghorne's superficially similar scheme.

Thus, while what follows has emerged in my own thinking from a more radical naturalism than Peacocke's, nothing in it is incompatible with the broad thrust of his approach. Indeed, it has drawn its inspiration largely from his work because it is rooted in a fundamental insight which is as intrinsic to Peacocke's approach as to my own: that no fundamental distinction should be made between different modes of divine action, of the kind inherent in the categories of supernatural/natural or personal/relatively deistic. In these latter category distinctions there is a strong implicit dualism in which any divine action that can be explored in terms of emergence through natural processes is demoted to a lower class in our thought. By contrast, both for Peacocke's model and for the version of the single-act account that I myself believe to be more coherent, this sort of classification is meaningless. Natural processes, in these views, are already in the first (and only) division, promoted to a far higher status than they have usually had in Western Christian thought.

This understanding is, it should be noted, intimately connected to a strand of Peacocke's thought that is quite separate from his reflections on the "causal joint" of divine action. This is his linking of the way he sees God acting through natural processes to the traditional Christian understanding of the nature of the sacraments. For there is, he says,

> a real convergence between the implications of the scientific perspective on the capabilities of matter and the sacramental view of matter which Christians have adopted as the natural consequence of the meaning they attach to Jesus' life and the continued existence of the Church. Briefly, it looks as though Christians, starting, as it were, from one end of their experience of God in Christ through the Holy Spirit acting on the stuff of the world, have developed an insight into matter which is consonant with that which is now evoked by the scientific perspective working from matter towards persons, and beyond.[30]

Peacocke himself uses the term *panentheism* (God in everything) to describe this understanding, but it might be better termed *sacramental panentheism* or *pansacramentalism*, in order to make clear that his attitude is far from the sort of pantheism in which God and the world are simply identified.[31]

The "Christian" insight into matter that Peacocke seems to take for granted in developing this view is not, however, one that is universally held within the Christian world. Such a positive view of the "natural" potential of the created order has, in fact, been manifested only rather rarely in Western Christianity. It is noteworthy, however, that though Peacocke only occasionally cites Eastern Orthodox theologians,[32] his sense of this potential finds its most obvious parallel in their conception of what Alexander Schmemann has called "The World as Sacrament." In this conception, as Schmemann notes, terms such as "sacramental" and "eucharistic" are cut free "from the connotations they have acquired in the long history of technical theology, where they are applied almost exclusively within the framework of 'natural' versus 'supernatural,' and 'sacred' versus 'profane,' . . ."[33] Quite independently of the Eastern Orthodox tradition, it would seem, Peacocke has developed an approach, which, like that tradition (according to Vladimir Lossky), "knows nothing of 'pure nature' to which grace is added as a supernatural gift," there being "no natural or normal state, since grace is implied in the act of creation itself . . . The world, created in order that it might be deified, is dynamic, tending always towards its final end . . ."[34]

Interpreted in terms of this kind of understanding, the type of *pansacramental naturalism*, which I advocate in what follows— essentially Peacocke's view of God's creative action, as outlined above, broadened to include providential action—is very far removed from the sort of theological naturalism advocated by people like Willem Drees, in which the natural world is viewed essentially through Enlightenment filters. While such a naturalism does, in Drees's work, lead to a recognition of "the richness of matter" in terms of "potentialities" that "have reached their climax so far in humans,"[35] it is unable to provide him with any way of exploring the significance of those potentialities, which is other than essentially humanist. The "richness of matter" is not interpreted, as in a pansacramentalist approach, in terms of an objective divine action. Instead, a recognition of the functional role that religions must have played in humanity's evolutionary survival leads Drees to a radical questioning of "the credibility of their references to a reality which would transcend the environments in which the religion arose."[36]

Such a questioning only becomes definitive, however, if we see the functional role of human religiosity as an inherently unpredictable "accident" in the evolution of humanity. This is often argued using the analogy of the view of biological evolution in which the present characteristics of the earth's species are held to be the fortuitous result of a series of highly improbable accidents. This latter view is, however, questionable. Recent genetic evidence has, in fact, pointed toward a very different idea, to what has been called "convergent evolution," according to which different evolutionary routes will, in a given ecological niche, tend to give rise to similar characteristics in genetically dissimilar species. According to this view, while there may be many potential evolutionary paths, no one of which is particularly probable, there will still be a broadly predictable destination.

This theory does not, of course, lead directly to the view that self-conscious, spiritually seeking beings are a predictable outcome of the nature of the cosmos. Nevertheless, it is certainly suggestive of such a possibility, especially when coupled with the speculation in recent years about what is usually called the Anthropic Cosmological Principle, which arises from the way the universe seems to be extremely "finely tuned" for the emergence of such beings.[37] At the very least, it allows us to see that the concept of the universe having some long-term aim need not be tied to a belief in the sort of quasi-vitalistic processes that are usually assumed in teleological accounts of the cosmos, and to see how a pansacramental naturalism may be explored explicitly in teleological terms. In this perspective, human religiosity can be seen both as forged by evolutionary pressures and divinely willed. The two are not incompatible.

One thing that becomes clear when these distinguishing characteristics of a specifically pansacramental naturalism are recognized is that it is entirely innocent of that implicit deism that some have claimed to perceive in it. While it is true that such a naturalism does have one characteristic that resembles eighteenth-century deism—the belief that God works out his purposes in and through the processes of the natural world—such a characteristic only provides an adequate definition of deism when interpreted in the context of a simplistic distinction between natural and supernatural, based on the concept of "pure nature."[38] This distinction was, indeed, exacerbated in eighteenth-century deism because of the mechanical and deterministic picture of the world in which it was then embedded. Other than in supernatural acts, God's only interaction with the world was, in such a framework, to design it and set its processes going. God was essentially no more than an "absentee landlord."

The approach that Peacocke has pioneered is, however, one in which the creative and evolutionary processes visible to the sciences—nondeterministic in scientific perspective and therefore genuinely open to creative novelty—provide the very locus of God's continuous activity. Thus, in the new perspective of the sciences of the twentieth century, a claim that God acts solely through the natural processes of his world in no way implies the absent God of deism. Rather, the model of God acting through the sacramental potential of his cosmos may be seen as fundamentally different from models based on a quasi-autonomous nature that, once created, either has no need of God, as in deism, or else requires supplementing by grace, which is "supernatural" in the sense of having no intrinsic connection to the grace inherent in the created order.

Nor, we should note, does a pansacramental naturalism have anything in common with the way the concept of revelation was ignored in eighteenth-century deism. Indeed, in Peacocke's general framework there is a strong implicit sense that it is not just human persons in themselves, but rather the revelation of God to such persons, that is the ultimate purpose for which the universe and its processes exist. There is no attempt to bypass revelation by means of a rationalistic natural theology or to interpret it as purely functional. Rather, as we shall discuss, Peacocke sees a proper theology of nature emerging authentically only when the natural world is viewed with the eyes of a faith engendered by response to revelation.

What Peacocke has begun to recognize, however, is that if revelation as a "given" must remain central to theology, a theology of nature based on the sacramental potential of the created order poses difficult questions about the traditional notion that "special" revelation comes about through a mode of divine action that either completely bypasses or else adds to the natural processes of the world. In his most recent work, in particular, there is a strong sense that the time has now come to examine how revelation, as an anthropological or psychological fact, can be integrated into the emerging picture of a God who acts in and through the natural processes of the world. "How," he asks, "does our understanding of God's interaction with the world including humanity relate to revelatory human experiences of God? How can the notion of religious experiences be accommodated by, be rendered intelligible in, be coherent with the understanding of God's interaction with the world that we have developed in the light of the perspective of science?"[39] While his previous work indicated that many aspects of divine action relate straightforwardly to the physical and biological sciences of the late twentieth century, the questions that he asks here are—as he himself seems to recognize—not so simple as those he has tackled previously.

Here, I would argue, the Barthian tradition's emphasis that revelation is only to be understood through its actual history must come into play. Without examining actual experiences that have the sense of being revelatory, considerations such as Peacocke's can, it would seem, provide no more than fascinating but vague speculations that, as Torrance has rightly suggested, will inevitably fail to be adequate to the nature of God's actual revelation of himself to the world. It is for this reason that we shall, in the next two chapters, turn entirely from the current science and religion debate and examine what Keith Ward has rightly called "the Christian paradigm of revelation"[40]: the resurrection. The type of task to which Peacocke's questions point us has, in this area, been more than half-completed. As we shall see, theological accounts of the Easter experiences that are able to provide the basis for a pansacramentalist understanding of revelation already exist.

3

The Easter Experiences:
An Incarnationist Approach

For some, the paschal proclamation "Christ is risen" receives its theological force from the supposed historical truth of the biblical accounts of the appearances of the risen Lord. For others, however, the redactional history of the resurrection appearance accounts is complex enough[1] to suggest that they certainly are not accurate records of actual experience, and may not even represent distorted echoes of such experience.

At one time it was fashionable to point to the echoes of ancient mythology and of the Hellenistic mystery religions[2] in the accounts in order to suggest that they were the product of a mythical accretion onto an originally somewhat vague perception of the spiritual reality of Jesus' continuing life. A similar view has recently been expressed in terms of aspects of current New Testament scholarship.[3] Against this type of view, however, others, while taking fully into account the problems associated with the New Testament narratives, have stressed the need to account for the astonishing transformation of Jesus' followers in the period following his death. The conversion of those followers—from a frightened and defeated group into the core of a confident and death-defying church—can, they suggest, be accounted for only by some direct experience.

Such a transforming experience need not, of course, have been of an empirical kind. Norman Perrin, for example, has argued from a historical perspective that the conversion experience of the Apostle Paul, as related by himself, provides the only reliable account of an encounter with the risen Christ, and as such provides the best available key to understanding the nature of earlier encounters.[4] If this is accepted, then the visionary nature of the Pauline experience inevitably leads to questions about those earlier experiences in terms of human psychology. Moreover, even if this argument is considered weak, a second approach exists that poses similar questions. A more conservative judgment about the subjective content of the Easter experiences is still susceptible to questioning in psychological terms. In particular, the striking parallels between the biblical accounts and the characteristics of certain types of visionary experience, as understood in Jungian psychology, strongly suggest the possibility of an imaginative, visionary explanation.[5]

While historical theologians have made several suggestions of this kind, however, systematic theologians have often been reluctant to engage with their conclusions.[6] There has, nevertheless, been a long tradition of exploration of important related questions. These were originally evoked in the late nineteenth century by the way the parallels between aspects of Christianity and of certain pagan religions, which had excited comment in early Christian times, were thrust once again into the limelight by the new flowering of anthropology and comparative religion. The effect of this was soon reinforced by an emphasis—characteristic of the period—on religious experience as such, and by the beginnings of the psychological exploration of that experience. While the reductionist anthropological and psychoanalytic models that first emerged in this climate were rightly dismissed as simplistic by theologians, the questions they had attempted to answer remained. Why was it, theologians felt bound to ask, that so much of the Christian faith seemed to be reflected in an apparently universal "natural religion"?

Among early responses to this question were those of Roman Catholic "modernists" of the early part of the twentieth century. Friedrich von Hügel, for example, with his particular stress on mysticism, attempted to construct a theological understanding that could do justice to both the objective and subjective elements of religious experience.[7] His friend George Tyrrell similarly struggled to find a way of talking about revelation in terms of his conviction that God communicated with humans in their wholeness and not through the intellect alone.[8] These early and interrelated attempts to formulate a model of God's revelatory activity were, however, premature in a number of ways, and not least because they were constructed in terms of a positivistic concept of scientific method.[9] (As we shall discover presently, this concept, with its emphasis on experimental verification, gave rise to a number of questionable theological emphases, not the least of which was the assumption of a rigid distinction between scientific and religious languages.)

If such attempts can be seen in hindsight to have been flawed, however, they can also be seen to have been full of important insights for the future of the theological discourse.[10] One of these, which has had long-lasting effects of permanent value, was a new emphasis on implications of the doctrine of the incarnation. That which was human, it was now increasingly stressed, was precisely that which God had taken to himself in Jesus Christ, so that human nature and culture should be seen as the very locus and focus of his saving acts. This type of "incarnationist" approach, in fact, became a commonplace in twentieth-century theology, and not only in the Roman Catholic community in which it began.

It stands in strong contrast to strands of thinking that see, in the doctrine of the incarnation, essentially no implications for an understanding of the created order. Whereas these latter traditions tend to see the myth of humanity's "fall" as implying an absolute gulf between God and his creatures, the incarnationist view tends to see it as delineating the way the empirical characteristics of humanity represent a distortion of what God had intended. Thus, human faculties in the fallen world are, for this incarnationist view, not irrelevant to salvation. Rather, they may be seen as constituting not only a vital part of the machinery through which salvation has been and must be brought about, but as part of the divine image in humanity restored as part of that salvation. As Louis Bouyer has put it, the human aspects of Christianity are important because the work of God is always the work "of a God who became man" so that "no matter how far the divine nature may transcend the human, the two cannot be described as being alien to each other. And even with greater reason they may not be conceived as being opposed. In the beginning, human nature was made in the image and likeness of God. Sin, it is true, disfigured this image and obscured this likeness. But the incarnation was to restore them."[11]

In many respects, this incarnationism may be seen simply as a restatement of the medieval concept of grace completing, rather than overturning, nature. Certainly, most of its proponents have, like Bouyer, been content to present it as such. What has been novel about much of its application since the late nineteenth century, however, has been the optimistic way in which "fallen" nature—before its transformation in and through Christ's incarnation—has been treated. Such optimism has less precedent in Western traditions than is often suggested and in certain respects may be seen as a development of doctrine rather than simply a restatement of it.[12]

As an example of this development, we may note that while earlier generations of scholars in Bouyer's tradition had tended to echo the strand of patristic writing that had seen, in parallels between Christianity and other religions, some sort of diabolically inspired caricature, Bouyer himself emphasizes quite another strand of the that tradition: that which "maintained that in the beliefs of all peoples could be found scattered seeds, as it were, of the *Logos,* of the Divine Word which finally flowered, full and united, into the Word made Flesh."[13] While acknowledging the possibility of diabolical caricature as an authentic component of a full understanding, Bouyer effectively neutralizes this possibility by arguing that it arises only because "God will not reveal Himself to man, and in man himself through the Incarnation, by causing him to renounce his own nature. It is by a more profound discovery of himself that man is able to discover, as in an impress, the divine visage and presence."[14]

It is, in fact, in the context of a recently developed incarnationist optimism about human religiosity that Bouyer is able to relate the Christian liturgical tradition to the psychological and anthropological models available to him. This enables him, for example, to affirm the apparent link between the beliefs and practices of Christianity and those of the Hellenistic mystery religions, by emphasizing how "the divine reveals itself in the transformation it effects in what is human."[15] He stresses that this need not imply either an underlying unity to which both can be reduced or some sort of historical causality. Rather, he argues, an incarnational approach makes the parallels between the two entirely understandable. (He feels the need to give warning to his readers, all the same, that a full recognition of what this means might leave them "astonished [at] how much man has put of himself into his belief in the supernatural, and how much God has accepted from Man so that he might give Himself to man in very truth.")[16]

If Bouyer's work may be seen as representing the mainstream incarnationist attitude to mythology as expressed in "natural religion," for a similarly mainstream incarnationist focus on the role of human psychology in religious experience we can look to the work of one who was one of the most influential theologians of the twentieth century: Karl Rahner. While Rahner, as we shall see, tends to avoid awkward questions about the psychological component of primary revelatory experience, he is the author of a profound and subtle essay on "private," secondary types of revelatory religious experience.

This is based in part on precisely the sort of incarnationist premise that we have seen in the work of Bouyer. "God as a free personal being," says Rahner,

> can make himself perceptible to the created spirit, not only through his works but also by his free, personal word. And he can do it in such a manner that this communication of God is not simply himself in the direct vision of the Godhead, or in the dimension of a blessed intellect emptied of all that is finite, but also, *and for a Christian who believes in God's incarnation this is essential*, in such a way that this communication is bound up with a particular place and time, with a concrete word or command, with a finite reality or truth, and so that it occurs with, or is connected with, an "apparition" of an object presented to the internal or external senses, which object represents and manifests God, his will, or the like.[17]

The basis of Rahner's approach is, however, not only a general understanding of the implications of the doctrine of the incarnation but also an appreciation of both the biblical witness and the experience of the mystics of the church. The details of this historical background, he says, should not only make the occurrence of visionary experience of divine origin obvious to the Christian, but also make it clear that such experience is usually of "created symbols," which vary widely "according to the phase of history of salvation in which the visionary lives and which he is intended to influence."[18] Indeed, Rahner continues, the concrete form of any such experience "may be conditioned in part by the historical milieu in which it occurs."[19]

Rahner goes on to address what he calls the psychological problem of visions, listing the traditional categorization of visions in the writings of the mystics of the Western church into three kinds: the corporeal, the imaginative, and the purely spiritual. Of these, he notes, the mystics themselves "regard the imaginative type as the more valuable and exalted!" and argues from this and a number of other observations that "the 'authenticity' of a vision cannot be simply equated with its corporeality, its objective presence within the normal sphere of perception affecting the external human senses."[20]

The problem of interpreting any vision of a person as a literal encounter with that person's real or even glorified body is, Rahner notes, considerable. "The fact that the object seen gives the visionary an impression of reality," he says,

> and is even integrated into the normal dimension of sense perception is no proof of the objectivity of the impression. For, on the one hand, we find the same thing in actual hallucinations and eidetic phenomena, and, on the other hand, this impression of accuracy is not a simple and immediate fact of consciousness but (as in the case of the simplest and most ordinary illusions) must be regarded epistemologically as a judgment which misinterprets the perception. . . . For the same reasons it is not to be taken as proof of the corporeality (and divine origin) of the vision if the person seen in it "speaks," "moves"—and even lets himself "be touched" (for even this happens in natural, purely imaginary processes); even if the visionary has the impression of learning something surprising and hitherto unknown to him. . . . It is always possible that the locution of a person seen in a vision may be the product of the creative subconscious of the visionary.[21]

Even in cases of more than one person experiencing a vision—some of which he clearly considers authentic—Rahner sees good reason to be skeptical of their corporeal nature. Noting that hallucinations are sometimes experienced by a number of people simultaneously, he simply recognizes such multiple experience as an aspect of human psychology (albeit still ill-understood)[22] and asks, as a theologian, "if . . . a psychic mechanism can be started simultaneously in a number of people, then the possibility that God too might make simultaneous use of these psychic potentialities in a number of people cannot be rejected *a priori*."[23]

Rahner's conclusion, on the basis of a number of lines of reasoning and in no way based on a reductionistic skepticism about the authenticity of religious visions, is that in most cases "authentic visions will be imaginative ones." However, he goes on, this statement does not solve the psychological problem of the nature of these visions but only poses it and indicates the direction in which a solution must be sought. Can we work out a more precise idea of imaginative visions? Two things can be said at the outset: on the one hand by the nature of the case such a vision must largely conform to the psychic laws determined by the intrinsic structure of the seer's spiritual faculties; and on the other hand, in order to be held authentic, the vision must be caused by God. (123)

The way that Rahner expands upon these two conditions manifests fascinating parallels with our earlier discussion of divine action through natural processes. While he is explicit that in his view God *can* suspend natural laws and produce visions that are miraculous in the sense of having an interventionist, supernatural input, he goes on to qualify this in a fascinating way. "Even where a miracle really occurs," he says,

> we can consider the laws of nature suspended only to the extent strictly required by the event; and in such cases as far as it is possible God will use the natural laws which after all he has created and willed. . . . Of course in an actual vision it will be almost impossible to trace the precise borderline between those psychical laws which necessarily operate and those which, though natural, are in fact suspended by the miraculous intervention of God. But if one considers . . . that miracles and their multiplication are not to be presumed but must be proved, then it is to be expected that even in visions of divine origin the seer's psychical structure and the laws of his nature will remain intact and operative to the fullest extent. (124)

As to the condition that the vision must be the work of God, Rahner makes a number of points. One is that in a sense everything (except sin) is the work of God, and that if an experience is of religious significance it is, "from the devotional point of view . . . immaterial whether the divine causality operates within or beyond the framework of natural law, since the religious man can rightly see, even in events that are capable of 'natural explanation', the free graces of God given for his salvation"(125). He then goes on to distinguish two categories of possible supernatural input. He observes that in addition to the technical miracle, involving a suspension of the laws of nature (including the normal laws of psychology), there is the type of act involved in the gift to individuals of what is sometimes termed "sanctifying grace." This, Rahner notes, is a "causality of God . . . which transforms nature but does not suspend its laws in any proper and empirically verifiable sense, which does not imply a merely sporadic divine intervention but belongs (even outside explicit Christianity) to the normal structure of concrete psychic reality" (126). In any actual case, he says, it will not be easy to say whether a vision is of supernatural origin in either of these senses or of both. Moreover, he notes, "the technically miraculous need by no means be more perfect, either ontologically or ethically . . . visions involving a partial or total suspension of natural laws must not on that account be considered 'corporeal' visions. They too can be and are purely imaginative ones" (127–28).

Rahner emphasizes, then, from a position of careful orthodoxy as far as his own Roman Catholic tradition is concerned, that authentic religious visions are usually imaginative rather than corporeal, and (by implication at least) are usually either entirely "natural," in the sense of being the product of the human psyche, or else supernatural only in the strictly technical sense of involving the influence of sanctifying grace which allows those laws to become unusually transparent to God's purposes. (This constitutes a type of "supernatural" input that, as we have seen, can easily be interpreted in terms of the pansacramentalism that we have noted in Peacocke's approach.)

The fact that Rahner does not explicitly apply these insights to the Easter experiences cannot, of course, be ignored. It would be entirely improper to suggest that he explicitly supports the contention that those experiences can and should be interpreted in terms of his analysis of secondary visions. The reasons for this seem to lie, however, at least in part in his apologetic desire to affirm the reasonableness of believing that God has, in Christ, made a "final and definitive revelation and self-disclosure" (98). For in his work not only, as one commentator has put it, are "historical details and hermeneutic fine points . . . subordinated to the one overriding concern, namely the demonstration of the possibility of being a Christian today without offense to one's rational nature."[24] In addition, as another has noted, Rahner often seems deliberately to avoid explicit historical application of his insights because of his fear of the "consequences of free floating research into the circumstances and intent of texts, etc."[25]

The argument for extrapolating Rahner's understanding of secondary revelatory experiences to primary ones does not, however, rest simply on a recognition of his apologetically motivated reticence. It is also arguable that such an extrapolation is implicit in much of his work. As Christopher Schiavone has observed, Rahner in practice "locates 'primitive revelation' (i.e., revelation from the Patriarchs to Jesus) in a broader history of revelation as a whole."[26] This comes about because, as Schiavone's penetrating study has shown, a central aspect of Rahner's framework is the belief that God's action on human beings is primarily at a contemplative level, which is deeper than that of either sensation or rational thought. Once we recognize that this contemplative dimension is, for Rahner, the very locus of God's revelatory activity, we can see that his analysis of secondary visions has at its heart an affirmation that, according to his general framework, may be equally applicable to primary ones. This is "that even in the imaginative vision it is not as a rule the vision as such (the stimulation of the sense organs) that is primarily and directly affected by God. Rather the vision is a kind of overflow and echo of a much more intimate and spiritual process ... the process which the classic Spanish mystics describe as 'infused contemplation.'"[27]

The legitimacy of applying this insight about imaginative visions to both primary and secondary revelatory experiences is suggested also by the way in which others, from within much the same tradition of theological thought, have made comparable analyses. Hans Urs von Balthasar, for example, manifests an approach that is similar to Rahner's in many ways, though it is more cautiously conservative, both in its stress on the ecclesial nature of religious experience and in its analysis of the content of such experience. This very conservatism allows von Balthasar, however, to apply an understanding of the imaginative nature of such experience to the Easter experiences themselves. Indeed, he sees those experiences as the actual basis for an affirmation of the psychological component of mystical vision. Because, he says, the "apparitions of the risen Christ to the Apostles were objective, even if they were not capable of seeing the fullness of his glory. There is then in principle no reason why the same, in essence, may not be true of mystical visions. The decisive factor is that the object . . . takes shape . . . in the spirit and senses of the mystic in a form that appropriately expresses and reveals it, and that, in so doing, the object can very well bring into play the mystic's own imagination."[28] Therefore, while von Balthasar, like Rahner, sees the actual content of any revelatory vision as essentially imaginative, his more conservative evaluation of what constitutes the objectivity of authentic visionary experience allows him to acknowledge a clear link between this insight and the nature of the Easter experiences.

In a parallel but rather more radical way, Edward Schillebeeckx has acknowledged the essentially imaginative nature of the visionary content of the Easter experiences. Indeed, in many of his comments, he has seemed to pay little or no attention to that visionary experience at all, stressing instead that the Easter experiences were primarily about the conversion of Jesus' followers to a new religious understanding. Nevertheless, in response to questioning, he emphasizes that it is not "necessary to deny visual elements in the Easter experience of the first Christians." On the contrary, he goes on, it would "be a mark of one-sided rationality if we were to remove all emotional aspects from this particular experience. Concomitant, even visual effects seem to have been ready to hand for these men within their culture."[29] Thus, whereas von Balthasar stresses the objectivity of the apparitions, seeing them as incomplete only insofar as human limitations required that the risen Christ took shape in an imaginative form that appropriately revealed his risen nature, Schillebeeckx goes beyond even the implicit Rahnerian view that I have outlined. He sees the visionary element not only as secondary in the sense of being an overflow of a contemplative encounter, but as "at most . . . an emotional sign of what really overwhelmed the disciples: the experience of Jesus' new saving presence in the midst of his people on earth."[30]

The witness of these three theologians makes clear that there already exists, within the broad incarnationist tradition, a spectrum of positions that relate to the psychological component of primary revelatory experience. Until now, however, even the most radical positions on that spectrum have manifested a relatively cautious attitude toward the "real" content of that experience and, at least implicitly, toward the question of what may be regarded as constituting authentic visionary experience. The possibility of an extension of the spectrum beyond this type of position has not been examined. Such an extension does emerge, however, from the answers that I shall offer to two questions that these earlier critiques have highlighted.

The first of these—of which Rahner in particular was very well aware—is that which we shall begin to examine in the next chapter. It is that of how the authenticity of any particular religious experience may be ascertained. The second, which we must leave until chapter 11, is that of whether and how the imaginative content of authentic religious experience refers directly to the divine reality from which it is assumed to originate. I shall suggest that persuasive answers to both of these questions can be found, provided that we remove the filters of a Christian exclusivism and begin to take seriously the revelatory experiences associated with the other faiths of the world.

4

Revelatory Experience and "Mere" Psychology

One of the chief problems of talking about an "imaginative" or "psychological" basis to revelatory experience is that most people in our culture instinctively interpret such terms in a reductionistic way. How, they immediately ask, is it possible to acknowledge the role of psychological mechanisms in revelatory experiences, and yet simultaneously to suggest that there is more to at least some of those experiences than psychology? To talk of psychology is, for them, to talk about "mere" psychology: it is to explain the phenomenon completely and to deny that it has any meaning or significance that is not expressible in purely psychological terms.

At one level, this sort of assumption often arises from a sort of socio-theological distaste for the "merely" human. As C. G. Jung remarks, in response to the adverse reaction to his own analysis of the psychic roots of religious experience, psychology "is spoken of as if it were 'only' psychology and nothing else . . . It smacks of blasphemy to think that a religious experience is a psychic process."[1] He goes on to comment, however, "How do we know so much about the psyche that we can say 'only' psychic? For this is how Western man, whose soul is evidently 'of little worth,' speaks and thinks. If much were in his soul he would speak of it with reverence. But since he does not do so we can only conclude that there is nothing of value in it. Not that this is necessarily so always and everywhere, but only with people who put nothing into their souls and have 'all God outside.'"[2]

There are, however, many Christians who would question the particular emphasis on God's transcendence—with its often implicit dualism—which has given rise to the attitude that Jung attacks. In particular, as we saw in the last chapter, analysis of religious experience in psychological terms has arisen quite naturally within incarnationist accounts of such experience, from which such dualism is largely absent. However, there can be no doubt that if one simply adopts the radical immanence of Jung's own approach to the psychic roots of encounter with the divine, one aspect of the problem voiced by critics of such psychological explanations remains. For even if we are inclined to accept Jung's belief that it is "only through the psyche that we can establish that God acts on us," there is a clear problem associated with acceptance of his further tenet that "we are unable to distinguish whether these actions emanate from God or the unconscious. . . . Both are borderline concepts for transcendental contents."[3] If accepted, this belief would seem to leave no way of distinguishing, in any objective sense, authentic from inauthentic manifestations of the divine.

For some, of course, this presents no problem. They are willing to accept the sort of relativism in which all religious experiences are equivalent—either all reducible to mere psychology or all equally valid instrumentalist encounters with some divine reality. The moment we ask whether some experiences should be deemed more authentic encounters with the divine than others, however, the question of the relationship between psychology and religious experience comes into sharp focus. What criteria, we must then ask, might allow a distinction to be made between, say, the Easter experiences, on the one hand, and encounters with UFOs or fairies, on the other, if all are seen as having a psychological dimension? Can we articulate criteria that allow only the first of these to be affirmed as both psychological in origin and revelatory of an extra-psychic reality? Or are we forced to reduce all such experiences to "mere" psychology?

The question of whether a reductionist methodology can be countered in this context will immediately, for some, call to mind the philosophical arguments currently heard about reductionism in the sciences. These arise from the way that, as Arthur Peacocke has noted, practitioners of some scientific discipline will often claim that another discipline, X, is "nothing but" an example of their own discipline, Y: "Thus X may be sociology and Y individual psychology; or X may be psychology and Y neurophysiology; or X may be neurophysiology and Y may be biochemistry; or X may be biology and Y physics and chemistry; and so the game goes on."[4]

As Peacocke goes on to note, however, this "ontological reductionism" of one level of description to another is not a straightforward corollary of the methodology of the sciences. He affirms wholeheartedly the latter: the "methodological reductionism" whereby any discipline seeks to understand the data of observation or experiment in terms of the discipline appropriate to the component parts of the system in question. As a biochemist himself, he is well aware of the fruitfulness of the study of biological systems in terms of the chemical properties of their components. However, he argues, this does not mean that biology is "just" chemistry applied to complex systems. Such an assumption about ontology is, he argues, dubious, for complex wholes cannot always be treated as nothing but the sum of their component parts.

Quoting philosophers of science who have none of his own apologetic motivation, he suggests that there is, at the very least, a "theory autonomy" whereby concepts needed to describe processes at a given level of complexity may not be reducible, even in principle, to concepts derived from a study of their component parts. From this fact, he argues that a hierarchy of descriptions is necessary, at each more complex level where new features may be seen as emerging, that cannot be described completely in terms of the properties at any lower level. Thus, he argues, just as aspects of living things cannot be described simply in terms of physics and chemistry (though without the need to posit any extra "ingredient," as is done in vitalism), so, for example, human consciousness can be seen as a "new emergent" at a higher level of complexity than simple life.

Many, on the basis of such arguments, now talk as Peacocke does of a hierarchy of complexity, which rises from those aspects of the cosmos properly studied by the physicist, through those studied by the chemist and biologist, to those which are the proper province of those who study the phenomena which are specifically human—the psychologist and sociologist. In this view, those engaged in studying one of the higher levels of complexity will rightly explore how the processes, observable and explicable by those studying lesser degrees of complexity, may contribute to (and sometimes explain fully) aspects of the level studied by their own discipline. Nevertheless, there may be aspects of that higher degree of complexity that, while needing no additional processes over and above those contributed by lower degrees of complexity, are not reducible to those processes. Rather, they require a recognition of autonomous emergent characteristics, possibly explicable ultimately in terms of "top down" organizing principles.

As the physicist Paul Davies has put it:

> There is no compelling reason why the fundamental laws of nature have to refer only to the lowest level of entities, i.e. the fields and particles that we presume to constitute the elementary stuff from which the universe is built. There is no logical reason why new laws may not come into operation at each emergent level in nature's hierarchy of organization and complexity. . . . It is not necessary to suppose that these higher level organizing principles carry out their marshalling of the system's constituents by deploying mysterious new forces specially for the purpose, which would indeed be tantamount to vitalism. . . . [Instead, they] could be said to harness the existing interparticle forces, rather than supplement them, and in so doing alter the collective behaviour in a holistic fashion. Such organizing principles need therefore in no way contradict the underlying laws of physics as they apply to the constituent parts of the system.[5]

Such an antireductionism on the part of some scientists has, understandably, been widely welcomed by theologians, since a thoroughgoing reductionism leaves no room for religion as anything other than an artifact of human culture, ultimately explicable in terms of "a structure in the nervous systems of millions of men the world over."[6] The possibility of the defense of theology that emerges from an antireductionist stance has, however, often been overstated and oversimplified. In particular, little has been said about the role of human psychology in religious experience, the implicit assumption apparently being that if religious experience and doctrine can at least in principle relate to something "more" than psychology, then any psychological exploration is redundant.

The opposite is in fact the case. Antireductionism in its most persuasive form is—as we have seen in the quotation from Davies— an approach that denies that the autonomy of some particular level in the hierarchy of complexity involves, at that level, any sort of process autonomy. Rather, while categories of description in a higher level of autonomy may not be reducible to those applicable to a lower level, and "top down" organizing principles may be at work, the processes at the lower level are always fully operative in the higher one and do not have to be supplemented by additional processes at the higher level.

Thus, just as biologists can legitimately claim, without being vitalists, that biology cannot be reduced to physics and chemistry, theologians might indeed be able to claim that their discipline need not necessarily be reduced to psychology. This in no way suggests, however, that psychological processes are not fully operative in the processes from which theology has arisen. Far more consonant with any argument from a scientific antireductionism would, in fact, be to view religious experience as emerging in and through psychological processes at the new level of complexity with which such experience deals.

This wider view has its own problems, however, which seem to have been largely overlooked by those who have explored it in a general way. For it often seems to be assumed that the possibility of defending theology in antireductionist terms is equivalent to putting the onus of proof onto those who believe theology to be reducible to psychology. It seems to be assumed that unless it can be demonstrated otherwise, there does exist, in reality, a level of complexity for which theology is the appropriate exploring discipline. For Peacocke, for example, theology is defensible in large part because of its position in the hierarchy of disciplines, one specified by its character of referring "to the most integrated level or dimension which we know in the hierarchy of relations." Thus, assuming that the relation of theology to other disciplines will be essentially that of any discipline to others that deal with less complex levels of reality, he suggests "it should not be surprising if the concepts and theories which are developed to explicate the nature of this activity are uniquely specific to and characteristic of it. As with other higher levels and dimensions, the concepts and theories theologians develop to describe this unique integration should not be prematurely reduced, without adequate proof, to the concepts and theories of the other disciplines appropriate to man, society and nature. For only detailed enquiry could establish which theological concepts and theories, if any, are reducible to (say) those of sociology and psychology."[7]

Peacocke's argument that theology *need* not be so reduced is not, however, logically adequate to demonstrate that it *should* not be so reduced. In the sciences, the onus of proof is still on the person who claims that at some level a genuine new emergent has arisen; if our argument in defense of theology is to be based on a scientific antireductionism, then the emphasis must surely be similar. If, therefore, Peacocke's analysis implicitly provides us with a way of thinking about the psychological component of religious experience in terms of emergence in and through psychological processes, it does not address the question of what makes it appropriate to affirm such emergence in particular cases. For, if some religious experiences are indeed "merely" psychological—as the religious experiences of some psychotic patients surely suggests—it is necessary to ask what makes for a reasonable claim that there are other experiences that, although arising through psychological processes, transcend the merely psychic.

The question is, then: If theological explanation of a particular psychologically rooted religious experience is not necessarily redundant, what makes it *appropriate?* Previously there have been two types of response to such questions. One has been to point to the historicity, realism, or self-authenticating numinous power of some particular experience. At its best, this type of response has tended to reflect the sort of understanding exhibited by C. S. Lewis, based on a rich appreciation of the mythmaking capacities of human beings. With his awareness of the clear relationship between the biblical witness to Christ and the myths to be found in many cultures, Lewis is forced to recognize both that the content of the gospels is "precisely the matter of the great myths"[8] and that this fact must be central to a theological understanding. Nevertheless, he argues, the very lack of "the mythical taste" in the gospels is a good indication that their mythical content arose not from a process of mythmaking in the usual sense, but from a direct experience of the mythical "facts." Only such direct experience, he suggests, can account for the way in which these facts were "set down in . . . artless historical fashion."[9] Thus, he concludes, "only here in all history the myth must have become fact."[10]

As it stands, however, this argument is a poor one. It would be equally applicable, for example, to the modern UFO phenomenon that, as C. G. Jung has shown in a fascinating psychological study,[11] bears many of the characteristics of explicitly religious "encounters" and has a comparable mythological rooting. Whether or not one accepts the details of Jung's particular approach, the general considerations that he sets out are sufficient to persuade us that direct, historical experiences of mythical form can occur without their being aspects of empirical reality. Lewis's version of the appeal to history is, therefore, unconvincing,[12] and indeed any appeal to history seems to stumble in the face of the possibility of psychological explanation.

As for the argument from the "self-authenticating" nature of true revelatory experience, this too seems susceptible to purely psychological explanation, especially when we take the plurality of faiths in the world with any seriousness, recognizing that experiences with these qualities are often mutually contradictory if taken as straightforwardly referential to some extra-psychic reality. Such qualities can clearly, in fact, be an intrinsic part of the psychological content of a religious experience. To claim validly that reductionism is improper clearly requires other criteria, which go beyond the nature of the religious experience taken in isolation.

One such possible criterion, emphasized by the second type of approach to the authentication of revelatory experience, is the presence of some sort of miraculous element in that experience. Richard Swinburne, for example, sees precisely this as the criterion for the authentication of revelation, stressing that by miracle he means, "a violation of the laws of nature, that is, a non-repeatable exception to the operation of these laws, brought about by God."[13] The approach that I have outlined, however, while it does not deny the highly unusual occurrences usually deemed miraculous,[14] eschews this definition of miracle precisely because it assumes the coherence of talking about divine action solely in terms of the natural processes of the cosmos. Unless, however, this model can provide an authenticating factor as clear as Swinburne's, at least in principle, then some might be tempted to judge his account the more coherent, despite the well-known problems of authenticating events as miracles in this supernaturalist sense.[15]

It is here, however, that parallels with the question of reductionism in the hierarchy of sciences are particularly instructive. For in arguing for the existence of an irreducible new emergent at, say, the biological level, what indicates that reduction to physics and chemistry is impossible is the irreducibly biological framework of the theory involved. This framework must be both genuinely explanatory and must necessarily be expressed in terms of biological, rather than physical or chemical, concepts. It is the coherence and explanatory power of new factors in the biological theory that gives rise to the claim that what that theory describes is more than just a special case of physics and chemistry, though there are no processes other than physical and chemical ones operative.

If we apply similar criteria to theology in relation to psychology, then it is clear that to sustain an antireductionist argument we must look at more than simply the religious experiences whose reducibility to psychology is in question. Just as in the biological case we must look beyond chemical processes to autonomous biological theory, so in the religious case we must look beyond revelatory psychological experiences to the doctrinal theory to which they give rise. Only if this doctrinal theory has adequate coherence and explanatory power, greater than that which could be provided by psychological theory alone, can we make a claim for the irreducibility of the processes from which it has arisen.

Thus, it would seem, once the intrinsic role of the psyche in religious experience is acknowledged, the question of the reducibility of that experience to psychology, unanswerable in purely historical or existential terms, must be tackled as an essentially philosophical problem in relation to the doctrinal structures that arise from that experience. That the psychological roots of religious experience *need not* imply a reductionistic analysis seems clear from the work of Peacocke. That they *should not* be understood in reductionist terms is still, however, to be demonstrated. Only, it would seem, through a rigorous philosophical analysis of the referential nature of doctrine will that be possible.

5

Revelation, Reference, and Rationality

The conclusion of the previous chapter presents two immediate problems for the theologian. The first is that by stressing that no revelatory experience has, within itself, any characteristic that is beyond explanation in psychological terms alone, it seems to turn upside down an aspect of the traditional reliance on revelation as primary and doctrine as secondary. It should be noted, however, that nothing I have said implies that revelatory experience is secondary to doctrine in either historical or existential terms. Indeed, I would stress that doctrine could not have arisen or continue to be accepted without a sense of its conformity to inner experience; like most contributors to the science and religion debate, I am skeptical of the claims of any natural theology maintaining that doctrine can be developed either from pure philosophy or from the observation of the world. Doctrine can arise authentically, I believe, only from the historical and existential "givenness" of revelatory experience.

For this reason, I think that it may be appropriate to continue to use the traditional term *special revelation* in relation to a psychological understanding of revelatory experience in order to indicate the *perception* of that experience as an undeserved "gift of grace." With that understanding, the term may thus be used to refer to exactly the same experiences as it is in a supernaturalist context, even though it is now interpreted as indicating not the non-natural character of the process by which these experiences come about, but rather the nonrational mode of their appropriation.

What makes this use of the term *special revelation* different from previous usage is that it is inherently tied, in an important way, to the concept of "natural religion." While it is true that there is nothing in this understanding of revelatory experience that resembles classical natural theology's simple movement from empirical observation to doctrine, the term *natural religion*, so long as we are very careful in our definition of it,[1] is entirely appropriate. The basic idea behind the concept of natural religion is that human beings, by their divinely willed nature, may have some degree of knowledge of God, or at least a capacity for such knowledge, quite apart from any supernatural acts of revelation.

The term as thus defined clearly includes natural theology based on the use of reason. However, natural capacity for knowledge of God is not necessarily limited to reason, but also embraces any non-rational natural human capacity for knowledge of God, such as that posited in a psychological model wherein religious experience arises from unconscious depths of the human psyche. If we are to use the term *natural religion* in this context, we must remember that the "nature" involved in such a natural religion is, for a pansacramentalist naturalism, far from being the autonomous nature of secular thought. To talk of the role of psychology in revelatory experience is not, in this perspective, to devalue revelation. Rather, it is to promote an aspect of our created being to a far higher status than it has usually had in Western theology. In this perspective, natural religion becomes, so to speak, an aspect of what we might call *natural grace*,[2] and "special" revelation as understood in terms of it remains a genuine gift of God, albeit one channeled through the sacramental potential of his cosmos rather than through supernatural means. What has changed is an understanding, not of the content of revelatory experience, but rather of the nature of the created order to which, and through which, that revelation is made.

The second major problem that arises from the conclusions of the last chapter is that of how revelatory experience is related to doctrine. In particular, we must grapple with the way that the old definition of revelation, as "disclosure or communication of knowledge . . . by a divine or supernatural agency,"[3] has come to sit uneasily with what many Christian theologians understand by the term. For two strands of argument—essentially independent, though often, in their effects, mutually supportive—have been instrumental in creating a climate of thought in which it is now widely thought anachronistic to hold that revelation legitimately gives rise to referential theological propositions.

One of these—that has had the greater influence in conservative Christian circles—has its roots in the theological and exegetical concerns of the so-called "Biblical Theology" movement, which was at the peak of its influence in the 1950s and 1960s. Proponents of this movement stressed what they called "revelation in history"—a phrase that, as James Barr observed,

> rose to prominence largely in reaction against the biblical inter-
> pretation of the "liberal" period in theology. It had then been
> common to depict a process whereby biblical man moved from a
> more "physical," "natural," and "tribal" view of God to conceptions
> increasingly more spiritual, elevated, ethical, and universal.
> Against this the later biblical theology . . . reacted strongly. The
> core of the Bible, it argued, was not a process of discovery or an
> advance towards higher conception; it was not an increasingly
> spiritual religion, but a revelation, through which God had made
> himself known to man. The medium through which he did so was
> not ideas or conceptions, however lofty, but historical acts, earthly,
> time bound, and contingent. . . . The argument thus directed
> against liberal theology was used also against old-fashioned con-
> servative theology: the revelation of God was not in statements or
> propositions, whether those of the Bible or of traditional theolog-
> ical documents, but in acts of history.[4]

Despite the manner in which the movement in its original form subsequently came under criticism,[5] a lasting result of it has been what David Kelsey has called a widespread consensus "that the 'rev-elation' to which scripture attests is a self-manifestation in historical events, not information about God stated in divinely communicated doctrines or concepts."[6] Sometimes this perspective has been expressed in an impressive and subtle form—as in the work of Yves Congar, for example, which we shall note presently. All too often, however, it has been taken rather uncritically to imply that the concept of information, even as a secondary aspect of revelation, has been discredited by conservative biblical scholarship.

It is important that we recognize, therefore, that from a philosophical perspective it is, as Richard Swinburne has noted, "very hard to see how God could reveal himself in history . . . without at the same time revealing some . . . truth about himself."[7] As we shall see, any concept of revelation in history that incorporates a psychological dimension will necessarily come to far more radical conclusions about the nature of that truth than does Swinburne himself.[8] Nevertheless, the general validity of his observation that "events are not self-interpreting"[9] must surely stand. While his own attempt to rehabilitate the concept of what he calls propositional revelation is open to questioning from a number of angles—and not least, as we have already noted, because of its reliance on a miraculous element—it points accurately to the way in which an affirmation that divine revelation is focused in historical acts does not preclude the inferring from those acts something of the character and intention of the agent.

This type of observation was largely obscured at the time that the concept of revelation in history became fashionable, however, because of a second line of attack on propositional understandings of revelation that already had a long history of association with instrumentalist analyses of the nature of religious language. At the time of the development of emphasis on revelation in history, this instrumentalist position was still usually based on the sort of naïve positivism that led many to attempt a complete separation of scientific and theological languages. (These were, admittedly, not always without merit. George Tyrrell's attempt to understand revelation in terms of a "model of interpersonal communication, which does not turn on experimental verification . . . but on shared meanings, situation, community of vision and action,"[10] for example, can be seen in some respects as a precursor of much that was fruitful in subsequent reflection on the nature of revelation.)

At the same time as at least some theologians became aware of the questionable nature of these positivistic assumptions, however, it became fashionable to attempt to justify an entirely instrumentalist understanding of theological language usage in terms of the Wittgensteinian concept of "language games."[11] Later still, as we shall discuss, a radical postmodernism, which seemed to point in much the same direction, was widely taken up in theological discourse. Neither of these developments meant, however, that assumptions rooted in an older positivism had evaporated; indeed, arguments supposedly based on Wittgensteinian or postmodernist insights are often flawed through the implicit or explicit use of them.[12] The reason for the confusion lies in part in the rather fragmentary account of developments in the philosophy of science over the past fifty or so years that many theologians have accepted.

It is, for example, widely and rightly recognized that there has been among philosophers a reevaluation of the Enlightenment notion of rationality, resulting in a radical modification of the once widespread belief that a straightforward foundation for human rationality exists, embodied in the scientific method. It is far from clear, however, that many theological commentators have fully understood the basis or content of this reevaluation. The critique of Enlightenment notions of rationality that occurred in this period is rarely, for example, seen other than in terms of the catastrophic downfall of the overblown claims of human reason. There is often little recognition that the undoing of these notions came about precisely through the development of broader views of rationality within the philosophical community.

The history of this development is a complex one, which may be said to have begun with the logical positivist attempt to give the Enlightenment view of rationality a greater degree of intellectual rigor than it had previously had. This was done through the assumption that, as far as the sciences were concerned, the only meaningful statements were those whose truth could be demonstrated by unambiguous appeal to sensory data. This meant, for the logical positivists, that not only should input from religion or metaphysics be proscribed, but so also should theoretical terms that could not be provided with correspondence rules to give them explicit phenomenal description. With this approach went an emphasis on what was called the verification of theories, it being assumed that the laws of nature could be derived simply, based on a collection of relevant data.

This attempt to establish the rationale of science was then arbitrarily extrapolated to become the rationale of all linguistic assertions and therefore of all knowledge claims. Thus, in what became the classic short exposition of the logical positivist position, A. J. Ayer could claim that theological statements were not simply wrong—in the sense that they could be contested by an atheist or by the proponent of a rival religious system—but were simply meaningless.[13] In the face of this kind of comment, it is hardly surprising that theologians were tempted to develop an account of theological language that denied that scientific and theological languages had any parallels.

By the time that Ayer was writing, however, there were already storm clouds on the logical positivist's horizon. One of the problems was that it was becoming clear that the sciences' fruitfulness was inextricably tied to the use of theoretical entities, which could not always be reduced to their observable manifestations in the way that the correspondence rules required. (This was related to the important question, to which we shall come presently, of whether the unobservable entities of theory—electrons, for instance—correspond, as the realists assert, to the ontology of the world, or are, as instrumentalists insist, simply useful ways of making predictions.) As if this problem were not sufficiently taxing for the logical positivists, another, and ultimately more destructive one, had also arisen. Some were beginning to ask: Can one really talk about verification at all? On the one hand, these critics pointed out, a given set of data is always compatible with more than one theoretical framework. The data that had apparently "verified" Newtonian physics by the end of the nineteenth century, for example, could now be seen as also compatible with the newer, relativistic physics of Einstein. If the data available were limited to what was available toward the end of the nineteenth century, there would be no way of choosing between the two theories, except perhaps in terms of economy and elegance, in which case the "wrong" theory—the Newtonian—would be chosen. How could this be understood in terms of the verification hypothesis?

Moreover, some were asking, is it really the case that scientific theory can be developed with no metaphysical input? As long ago as the eighteenth century David Hume had insisted that a generalization could not be proved on the strength of examined instances without using unproved premises. More and more, the logical positivists were having to admit that such premises were indeed intrinsic to their argument, and defending them, not in terms of irrefutable logic, but simply in terms of apparent probability. (One such "probable" assumption, for example, is that the future will be like the past—an assumption that, as Bertrand Russell once pointed out, will eventually fail for the chicken who, accustomed to being fed every morning, finds that on Christmas Eve it has its head chopped off instead.)

The downfall of logical positivism came, however, not from the cumulative effects of progressive modifications of its tenets in the face of the minutiae of philosophical analysis. It came instead from the widespread acceptance of a number of new analyses of the methodology of science, each of which contained powerful arguments against the logical positivist scheme.

The first of these was that of Karl Popper,[14] which, had it been translated into English immediately after its publication in 1934, might well have prevented logical positivism from ever developing the stranglehold that it had on English-speaking philosophy around the middle of the twentieth century. However, it was not for another twenty-five years that those unable to read the German of the original edition could become aware of the way that Popper had changed not simply the answers to the old questions about scientific logic, but the questions themselves.

It is not verification that is the issue in scientific development, Popper suggests, but falsification. The search for new theories he argues, always arises from new data that do not fit accepted theories, and thus "falsifies" them. A new theory, to be acceptable, has to explain both the old data, which do not challenge the old theory, and the new data that do. Therefore, while he shares with the positivists the conviction that science is a logical activity, he in effect turns the positivist program on its head by locating the essential feature of rationality in criticism rather than in justification, and substituting falsification for verification, theory for observation, and fallibilism for probability.

This Popperian scheme—especially in revised versions that have dealt with some of its initial oversimplifications—has had considerable appeal for many theologians as the basis for understanding the nature of theological statements and for defending their rationality.[15] A theological appropriation of the Popperian scheme did not, however, prove to be without its problems. While that scheme effectively demolished the logical positivists' framework, its emphasis on falsifiability did not unambiguously serve the interests of those who wished to argue for the rationality of theology. Indeed, before the translation of his seminal work into English, English-speaking philosophers, under the sway of a diluted version of logical positivism, had already used a comparable criterion of falsifiability to claim that theological language was meaningless.[16] They argued that while religious believers often seem willing to modify their theology in the face of new evidence or argument, nothing, it seemed, can conceivably make them recognize that their faith as a whole has been falsified. In the context of Popper's own early work, this argument still seemed to have some validity; one of the main problems with was that it failed to recognize the way that discordant data, which could not be explained in terms of a current theoretical framework, did not, in actual scientific practice, always bring about that framework's downfall. Only considerably later, in the work of Imre Lakatos,[17] was a quasi-Popperian way of analyzing this fact developed, in terms of a distinction between core theories—which are given up only extremely reluctantly—and auxiliary hypotheses, different possible changes that can be explored in competing research programs.

This Lakatosian modification to Popper—subsequently taken up and applied to theology by Nancey Murphy[18]—was, however, only one of many that followed in the wake of another challenge to the positivist conception of scientific rationality that made Popper's own seem tame. For only a very few years after Popper's work had become widely available through its translation into English, his basic approach, which had attempted simply to develop a new understanding of the logic of science, was challenged root and branch by that of Thomas Kuhn.[19] Not only did Kuhn's arguments effectively bring an end to talk of scientific "logic" as such; they seemed at the time to challenge even the basic rationality of the scientific enterprise. This came about through his focus on radical theory changes, of the type that he termed "paradigm shifts." According to Kuhn, such a shift—the change from Newtonian to relativistic physics, for example—is not simply a progression from one theoretical framework to another, based on a simple set of logical rules applied to experimental or observational data. Rather, he suggests, the process is inevitably far more complex, in that a paradigm is not simply a set of accepted formal theories, but a framework of thought and practice inculcated by standard examples of problem solutions in a field.

Such a paradigm, according to Kuhn, involves not only the acceptance of a certain set of theories and practices, but also a certain domain of data that are interpreted in terms of the paradigm, there being no independent pool of data that can provide a simple, logical means of choosing between competing paradigms. This "theory laden" characteristic of data means, for Kuhn, that the shift of a scientific community from one paradigm to another is not a simple matter of obedience to a "logical" set of rules, but rather a matter of a gestalt-type conversion, in which the world is seen in a new way. Thus, he argues, proponents of competing paradigms suffer from "incommensurability"—an inability not only to agree on the relevance and weight to be accorded to particular data, but even to speak about that data in the same language.

Kuhn's analysis has evoked a heated debate about the basic rationality of science. Some, like Paul Feyerabend, have gone much further than Kuhn himself, arguing that "the events, procedures and results that constitute the sciences have no common structure,"[20] and asserting the merits of what has been called a radical opportunism as far as setting up research programs is concerned. Others, taking up important and undoubtedly valid aspects of the sociology of knowledge, have argued that the recognition that aspects of scientific practice are susceptible to sociological analysis must lead to the (reductionist) conclusion that any given paradigm is "merely" a social construction.

The majority of commentators within the philosophy of science have, however, reacted to Kuhn's approach not by attempting to be even more radical, but by attempting to incorporate what are widely seen as his genuine insights—about the theory laden nature of data, for example—into a framework wherein a basic scientific rationality can be defended. In practice, the majority of current philosophers of science, despite their divergent approaches, are in agreement that the denial of the rationality of science, which became fashionable in the immediate aftermath of the Kuhnian analysis, is at least as simplistic as the type of facile rationalism to which that denial was a reaction.

While it is now universally accepted that the old search for straightforward rules governing the logic of scientific activity can never be resumed, it is at the same time widely denied—by those who have looked closely at the issues—that the concept of scientific rationality has become invalid. (Admittedly, the Enlightenment overtones of the term *rationality* have led some to use alternative terms such as *entitlement* or *justification*.)[21] While it is recognized that the positivist and Popperian attempts to define that rationality in terms of logical rules was ultimately a failure, and that the attempt to articulate "foundational" rational beliefs to function as the basis of scientific knowledge must be abandoned, it is still widely affirmed[22] that scientists act as rational agents, and that the extraordinary success of the sciences can only be understood in terms of their rationality, even though this rationality must be understood in terms of much richer patterns of thought and language than can be captured by the rules of traditional logic.

This majority movement within the philosophy of science has often been understood somewhat simplistically by theologians. On the one hand, many of those involved in the science and religion debate have effectively ignored the way that the views of Kuhn and his successors really have undermined the old "foundationalist" understanding of rationality in a radical way. As a result, when defending the rationality of theology and discussing its language usage, they have tended to adopt Popperian stances and to emphasize similarities between the disciplines at the expense of differences, concentrating on methodological parallels between the two disciplines and often also (as we shall see presently, when we look at this stance in detail) developing a simplistic—if still fruitful— understanding of the referential nature of their languages.

This has certainly been useful in challenging the assumptions of those who, because of their positivistic assumptions, see theological language purely in instrumentalist terms. It has been fruitful too in its quasi-Popperian emphasis that future development of theory will inevitably modify current usage, so that even those who cling to a foundationalist concept of rationality now widely accept that theological language can do no more than represent an inherently provisional reflection on acts of divine revelation. (When, for example, they look at Swinburne's critique of the common understanding of the concept of revelation in history, they interpret his suggestion that any revelation in history must be expressible in propositional form in a more nuanced way than he himself does, recognizing that any such propositional form cannot be equated in a simplistic way with "propositional truth." Rather, they see any propositions that are enunciated through reflection on revelatory experience as representing, at best, provisional and revisable models of the reality to which they refer.)

If those who have been reluctant to give up foundationalist assumptions about rationality have thus often had a beneficial influence on general theological discourse, the same cannot be said for those contemporary theologians who, when discussing the nature of their discipline, have uncritically accepted certain "postmodernist" accounts of the nature of rationality in the wake of the downfall of foundationalism.

J-F Lyotard's account of the methods, goals, and achievements of the natural sciences, for example, seems to be taken for granted in certain theological circles. As Alister McGrath has observed, however, that account is "simply not taken seriously within the scientific community, nor by many others outside it."[23] Apart from anything else, it is simply not descriptively accurate. As McGrath notes in a quotation from Steven Connor, "Lyotard paints a picture of the dissolution of the sciences into a frenzy of relativism in which the only aim is to bound gleefully out of the confinement of musty old paradigms and to trample operational procedures underfoot in the quest for exotic forms of illogic. But this is simply not the case. If some forms of the pure sciences . . . are concerned with the exploration of different structures of thought for understanding reality, then this still remains bound, by and large, to models of rationality, consensus and correspondence to demonstrable truths."[24]

If many theologians have failed to sail between the Scylla of foundationalism and the Charybdis of irrationalist postmodernism, however, proponents of a theological "postfoundationalism" have been able to point to important epistemological nuances in an exploration of the relationship of science and religion. Of these, it is perhaps J. Wentzel van Huyssteen who most clearly expounds the possibility of the sort of middle way that the rest of this essay attempts to explore. He argues that while a valid postfoundationalism must deny any simplistic notion of rationality based on one particular field of intellectual endeavor, it need not lead to a position in which the many fields of intellectual endeavor have "many rationalities" with no points of contact. Scientific reflection remains, he suggests, "possibly our best available and clearest example of the cognitive dimension of rationality at work . . . [so that] contemporary philosophy of science still forms the most important epistemological link in the current science and religion debate."[25]

Van Huyssteen acknowledges that while one can not justify "any claim that uncritically extends the nature of . . . a strictly scientific rationality to the rationality of religious or theological reflection,"[26] one can still argue that

the rationality of science and the rationality of religious reflection do seem to overlap at some very crucial junctures. The theologian shares with the scientist the crucial role of being a rational agent, of making the best possible rational judgments within a specific context and for a specific community. The theologian also shares with the scientist the fallibilism implied by the contextuality of rational decision making and thus the experiential and interpretative dimension of all our knowledge. The experiential and interpretative roots of religious knowing are, however, much more complex than the mostly empirical roots of scientific knowledge. Rationality in religion and in theological reflection is, therefore, a broader and more complex affair than a strictly scientific rationality. . . . The lingering imperialism of scientific rationality should not close our eyes, however, to the remarkable epistemic consonance between scientific and theological ways of thinking.[27]

Important aspects of what van Huyssteen points to in these comments are clarified not only by his own arguments but by looking more carefully than is often done at previous analyses of the epistemological overlap between theology and the sciences, even when these have in some respects exemplified the approach that van Huyssteen criticizes.[28] Ian Barbour's discussion of the application to science and theology of the concepts of coherence, scope, and fertility, for example, may be seen in a postfoundationalist context to have been not so much superceded as brought into clearer and more nuanced focus.

A theological coherence criterion, for example, may arguably still be explored in terms of the way in which, as Ian Barbour has put it, a scientific theory should "be consistent with other accepted theories and, if possible, conceptually interconnected with them," exhibiting also internal coherence and "simplicity of formal structure, smallest number of independent or *ad hoc* assumptions, aesthetic elegance . . . and so forth."[29] Indeed, a coherence criterion of this sort constitutes one of the main motivations for the interpretation of divine action in terms of pansacramental naturalism that I have outlined. One of the main advantages of such an interpretation is precisely that it allows such things as revelation and providence to be understood *within* an understanding of creation, rather than as essentially arbitrary additions to it.

Similarly, the concept of scope will be of central importance to what follows. As Barbour has indicated, scope in the scientific context means that theories "can be judged by their comprehensiveness or generality. A theory is valued if it unifies previously disparate domains, if it is supported by a variety of kinds of evidence, or if it is applicable to wide ranges of the relevant variables."[30] This he sees as being applicable to religious belief in so far as theological models "can be extended to interpret other kinds of human experience beyond the primary data," noting that in a scientific age "they must . . . at least be consistent with the findings of science."[31] As we shall see, the view of the role of theological language that I shall develop takes this concept of scope with great seriousness, although in a postfoundationalist context.

In the same way, fertility—which Barbour characterizes in terms of a theory's promise to encourage an ongoing research program[32]—will be an important characteristic of all that follows. As we shall see, a wide-ranging program of this type is precisely what my arguments suggest.

6

Revelation as "Data"

If a postfoundationalist approach allows us a more nuanced understanding of the concepts of coherence, scope, and fertility, this does
not mean that these concepts in themselves are adequate to explore
the rationality of theological discourse. It is, in fact, relatively easy to
show that a wide range of theological approaches are comparable
with other rational disciplines in relation to these qualities. Such
comparability cannot in itself, however, demonstrate that any of
those approaches involve reference to what Peacocke (as we saw in
chapter 4) has called "the most integrated level or dimension which
we know in the hierarchy of relations."[1]

Such a demonstration requires not general assertions about
methodological comparability, but detailed argument that a *particular* theology is a coherent and appropriate response to the total
(including revelatory) human experience of the cosmos. As van
Huyssteen has put it, being rational in both theology and science is

> not just a matter of having some reasons for what one believes in
> and argues for, but having the strongest and best available reasons
> to support the rationality of one's beliefs within a concrete con-
> text. The hazy intersection between the diverse fields of theology
> and the other sciences is therefore not in the first place to be deter-
> mined by exploring possible methodological parallels or degrees
> of consonance between theology and science. What should be
> explored first is a common and shared resource found in a richer
> notion of human rationality.[2]

A major aspect of the "richer notion of human rationality" of which van Huyssteen speaks is, I would argue, the recognition that evidence or data may have quite different characteristics in different areas of intellectual endeavor. This means that the issue of what is usually (and simplistically) called "agreement with data"—the fourth quality of any rational discipline as outlined by Ian Barbour—becomes a complex one in which the postfoundationalist insistence that no one discipline can be taken as the paradigm of rationality is of the greatest importance.

This means that, as far as theology is concerned, we must not only take into account Barbour's own comment that theological data "are much more theory-laden than in the case of science" so that we must "examine the influence of beliefs on experience"[3]—though, as we shall see, this is crucial in any psychological understanding of revelatory experience. We must also recognize that there is in fact a complex, two-way interaction of experience and doctrinal understanding, of the type noted by van Huyssteen when he argues (in the wake of some important observations by William Stoeger)[4] that the difference between science and theology "is not . . . based only on the difference between 'empirical problems' and 'God's revelation.' The difference between the two is a much more refined one, and is found rather in significant differences in *epistemological focus, experiential scope*, and *heuristic structures*."[5]

It is important to note, however, that such differences exist among the sciences as well as between science and theology. Here, it would seem, we can learn much from Philip Clayton's argument that important aspects of the distinctiveness of theology are clarified by seeing it as lying at one end of a methodological spectrum. At the other end of this spectrum, Clayton suggests, is physics, while intermediate positions are occupied by disciplines that deal with intermediate levels of complexity. In particular, he argues that the data and models of the social sciences may be seen as an important bridge between physics and theology.

This bridge arises, Clayton explains, from the way that philosophers of the social sciences, such as Jürgen Habermas, have often stressed that the social world, in which the discourse of researcher and researched takes place, must be intuitively grasped if adequate explanation at the social level of complexity is to be possible. Many of them sum this up in terms of the concept of "understanding" (*verstehen*), without which, as Clayton has noted, no informed collation and explanation of relevant data will be possible, since "one must get to this theoretical level without falsifying the subject matter in question." Because of this, Clayton continues, understanding is a necessary precondition for social scientific explanation, and "to the extent that understanding is hampered or incomplete in regard to a given range of phenomena, the probability of explaining those phenomena adequately is reduced."[6]

Clayton then extrapolates this insight to the study of religious beliefs, saying that just as in sociological or anthropological theorizing, "so also one precondition for adequate theories of religion is some *understanding* of the religious dimension . . . This may include some personal religious experience, though this is not in itself sufficient and may not even be necessary. Also required is an openness to believers' ways of thinking and perceiving and a willingness to consider religious phenomena nonreductionistically."[7] (Clayton's insights here point to much that is wrong with analyses of religious belief from the pens of hardened atheists such as Richard Dawkins.)[8]

This analysis of a methodological spectrum from physics to theology points also, it would seem, to some important points about data in the narrower "empirical" sense. The distinction between quantitative and qualitative data that is sometimes held to separate the data of theology from that of science, for example, is often ill considered. It arises from the common mistake of defining proper scientific practice in terms of physics, the most quantitative of the sciences. (It is clearly true, for instance, that the physicist's statement that a theory makes adequate quantitative sense of the data, within experimental error, has no theological equivalent.) The way that the data of physics is quantitative is not, however, indicative that there must be something "rationally" wrong with the data or method used by researchers into higher levels of complexity. Because the physicist deals with reality at the lowest level of complexity, the quantitative study of particular phenomena, both experimentally and theoretically, is relatively straightforward. Even in biology, however—still a relatively "hard" science—there are necessary concepts such as predator and sexuality that are essential components of certain data and yet are difficult or impossible to quantify. By the time we have moved to disciplines that deal with even higher levels of the hierarchy of complexity, such as sociology, there is not only much that is beyond quantitative analysis, but also, as noted above, much more difficulty in formulating interpretative schemes.

Examination of the whole range of disciplines that have a claim to using a rational methodology suggests, in fact, that rather than defining the nature of good data and its use in terms of the science that deals with the lowest level of complexity, that underlying rationality must be understood in terms of the way it will manifest different characteristic methods and conceptual schemes at different levels of complexity. The question of the rationality of a discipline thus becomes not how well it corresponds in methodology to that of physics, but of whether it appropriately provides genuine insight into the level of complexity under investigation.

A similar analysis can be applied to the common appeal to the repeatability of scientific experiment or observation, which is often contrasted with theology's supposed reliance on unrepeatable and unique historical events. Once again, this appeal is often based largely on seeing physics—the experimentally based search for time-independent laws at the lowest level of complexity—as the science *par excellence*. This makes it easy to forget that some branches of the natural sciences do concern themselves with unrepeatable events in the history of the cosmos. Some of these, such as the "big bang" from which the cosmos emerged, are in principle unrepeatable (unless the universe oscillates as some cosmologists suggest, but even if this were the case no observer in this universe could survive to experience a repeat). Others, such as the emergence of particular species, may in principle be repeatable but in practice are certainly not so. It may be true that the scientific theory related to unrepeatable events originally developed largely from repeatable observations, but it is equally true that these historical events and processes now form part of the theory that affects data interpretation.

Nor should we necessarily assume that revelatory phenomena are in principle unique. If, for example, intelligent beings exist elsewhere in the universe—as is certainly possible and even likely from a scientific perspective—it hardly seems necessary, even from a conventional supernaturalist standpoint, to insist that they must wait for contact with the human inhabitants of the earth before having access to the revelation involved in the incarnation of Jesus. (A widely used modern hymn by Sydney Carter suggests, certainly, that a parallel incarnation for each separate intelligent life-form is not to be ruled out.)[9] It would seem that, even from a conventional standpoint, the historical uniqueness of a revelatory event may be thought of as more related to the *de facto* uniqueness of the environment than to anything intrinsic to the phenomenon. (As we shall see in chapter 11, this viewpoint may be expressed in terms of a pansacramental naturalism in a particularly simple way.)

This type of blurring of conventional distinctions between the data of theology and the sciences should not, however, blind us to one vital distinction. Although two investigators in a scientific discipline may, as we have noted, suffer from incommensurability, so that the data that they consider relevant may not only be different but may also be expressed in mutually incomprehensible theoretical languages, the proponent of one paradigm can still ask the other a question like this one: "Given this apparatus, set up in this way, does your theory have an explanation for the way the pointer of this dial points to this mark on its surface?" (While this particular example uses the language of the lowest level of complexity, equivalents can be constructed for higher levels.) There is, for both investigators, a world that is in some sense independent of their theoretical perception of it, in that both can agree, if they have the gift of sight, that the pointer does precisely what it does. Even Feyerabend—often held up as the prime proponent of scientific irrationality—has recognized that no degree of incommensurability can preclude mutual criticism of theories in such a situation, even if the interpretation and significance of the observation in question are matters of dispute.[10]

In theology, by contrast, no comparable appeal can be made in relation to revelatory experience. Even those who undergo some revelatory experience may, as we have seen, validly wonder whether it is no more than a psychological artifact. More importantly, those without religious faith—and, indeed, those of a different religious faith—have no reason for taking the revelatory "raw data" provided by a religious believer seriously as referential to some "external," divine realm of being. Indeed, given the variety and apparent mutual incompatibility of such data, it would seem foolish for them to do so. Just as a blind person would rightly question the nature of physical sight if it happened that all the observers of the pointer experiment outlined above reported different outcomes, so the nature of religious "sight," given its mutually incompatible "sightings," also requires questioning.

It is precisely here that a theological understanding of revelation as providing something more than data is of crucial significance. In particular, in relation to both a psychological model of revelatory experience and the concept of revelation in history, the widespread theological assertion that revelation is not to be seen *primarily* in terms of reference to, or information about, a divine reality is of considerable importance.

The work of two theologians seems to be particularly relevant in this respect. The first of these is Yves Congar,[11] who has attempted to incorporate genuine insights from the revelation in history approach into a broader and deeper theological understanding than has been manifested by most of its proponents. The most important characteristic of Congar's approach is, perhaps, his emphasis that God makes himself known not in abstract knowledge but in "signs," which are always oriented primarily toward salvation, being "proportionate to our human condition" and couched "in the language of men, in images, concepts, and judgments like our own."[12] He sees the content of these signs as having a genuine ontological content,[13] but this must, he insists, be expressed in terms of "mysteries," which are partially hidden truths, made present most fully in the liturgical celebration of salvation, and always, when expressed linguistically, to be approached apophatically.

Since for Congar all revelation is of God himself and tends toward a final, eschatological fruition, he talks of an "economy of the disclosures of God" in terms of three "unveilings of our eyes" that correspond to Aquinas's sequence of law, grace, and glory. The first of these relates to what may be known of God by reason, the second to faith in relation to revelation in history, and the third to the eschatological vision of the blessed. As William Henn has observed, not only does this perspective "fit nicely into Congar's historical approach to truth," but also "the view that revelation is progressive and will be completed only at the eschaton serves as a major limiting principle with regard to the adequacy of any present statements which intend to convey revealed truth. All such statements, in principle and by their very nature, must be treated in sober manner, which is aware of their 'proleptic,' provisional and not-fully-adequate nature."[14]

The main importance of this approach lies, I would suggest, in its attempt to give a theological exposition of how revelatory experience does far more than simply refer. Revelation, Congar always stresses, "does not attempt to make us knowledgeable about what God is in the way in which we are knowledgeable about the chemical composition of the body, but rather seeks to show us the true religious relationship with God."[15] This is important here because it is in the light of this type of understanding that the arguments about the referential content of revelatory experience, which will take up much of the rest of this essay, should be understood. If a reaction to much of the recent thinking about revelation has led me to stress referential content at the expense of other aspects of the revelatory process, this is not because I believe that such reference is its only or even its most important characteristic.

Indeed, one argument for stressing the unconscious, rather than cerebral, component of revelatory experience, in the way that I have so far, is precisely that the instrumental effectiveness of such experience transcends that which would come about through the conveyance of information alone. This implies the importance of mechanisms involving the totality of the human psyche, not simply those involving its conscious component. The question of reference is thus only one aspect of revelation seen in terms of divine action through a psychological mechanism.

If our understanding of revelatory experience is to combine this concept of psychological mechanism with that of referential content, however, it is important that we avoid the sort of simplistic model sometimes assumed by theologians, in which a "universal" human psychology, essentially independent of the individual's history and culture, is seen as the medium of God's revelation. That there is a component of human psychology that is indeed universal in this sense need not be doubted, for as we have noted in relation to Drees's type of naturalism, humans do have a common evolutionary history that will inevitably provide the rooting for human religiosity. As we observed, however, this is less definitive for an understanding of that religiosity than is often assumed. A psychological theory based on such an evolutionary perspective would, in fact, be easy to incorporate in a referential understanding of revelation: the psychological dimension could become simply an appropriate "hosepipe" for the conveyance of information, acting as a sort of quasi-Kantian filter through which it is apprehended.

As a psychological theory, however, such an approach would surely be inadequate. For even those theories, such as the Jungian one, which posit an important component of the human psyche that is indeed independent of the individual's history and culture, are far from assuming that this component is all that need be considered in analysis of psychological experience. Cultural and historical specificity remain, in such theories, of prime importance,[16] which suggests that, in any model of revelatory experience with a psychological component, such specificity must be taken fully into account.

It is for this reason that, despite all that it has to recommend it, Congar's concept of revelation must be seen as ultimately inadequate. Despite the great strengths that arise from its appropriation of the concept of revelation in history, and its subtle recognition of the interplay of psychological factors and the objectivity of God's self-revelation in relation to salvation, its psychological insight is essentially of this "hosepipe" character.[17] In this respect, Congar's account is inferior to that of Rahner who, if far less historically minded than Congar in general, was, as we have seen, aware of the way in which the "concrete form" that (at least secondary) divine revelation takes "may be conditioned in part by the historical milieu in which it occurs."[18]

In particular, an openness to the possibility of cultural conditioning in revelatory experience inevitably poses the question of how the experience might occur in cultures that do not share the assumptions of Judaism or Christianity. It is for this reason that the second theologian whom I wish to cite in relation to the concept of revelation is of considerable significance. Keith Ward's attempt at a pluralist model of revelation, while in certain ways very different in emphasis from that which I wish to develop, clearly acknowledges this factor. He stresses, for example, that the very diversity of religious traditions implies that revelation should not be seen in terms of the gift of direct divine knowledge, but rather in the light of a concept of God "communicating within the framework that societies have themselves developed. . . . Not only does God use the natural language of a people; God uses their thought forms, their characteristic modes of expression, and their penumbra of tacit connotations and resonances."[19]

His particular focus is, moreover, one that complements my own on foundational and nonrational revelatory experience, in that it is based on the communities of faith that have emerged from such experiences and on the verbal aspects of the development of their doctrinal frameworks. Thus, for example, in relation to non-Christian traditions, he strongly emphasizes prophetic utterance, developing a "view of revelation as a Divine shaping of human thoughts in particular cultural and historical contexts."[20] Moreover, in relation to Christianity, he seems to be strongly influenced by that potent (and entirely legitimate) tendency of recent Christian thinking that stresses that revelation should not be thought of simply in terms of individual acts or experiences, however important, but rather in terms of the entire process by which the community of faith has come to its common understanding. This means, for example, that the Christian revelation, though focused on the person of Jesus Christ, has to be seen in terms not only of his life, death, and resurrection, but also in terms of the way in which, under the inspiration of the Holy Spirit, the community of faith developed, among other things, a canon of scripture and a common doctrinal framework.

The psychological considerations, which have constituted an important component of my argument so far, suggest, however, that Ward's analysis is incomplete because it lacks proper emphasis on nonrational revelatory processes in general and on foundational revelatory experiences in particular. While he is undoubtedly right to stress that the revelatory process involves "objective Divine action and personal liberation . . . human experience of encounter and of union . . . [and] reflective and imaginative interpretation,"[21] his lack of emphasis on the second of these components is striking. Although he examines the Christian revelation at some length, for example, he makes little or no attempt to discuss the way in which Jesus' own disciples came to belief in him as the risen Lord, or to the related question of how the modern Christian comes to the belief that the proclamation of that primary experience is to be accepted as authentic.

If a failure to emphasize that revelation usually begins through nonrational mechanisms means that Ward's approach remains one-sided, however, his general considerations undoubtedly provide an important complement to those outlined here. In particular, the more fruitful aspects of his model emphasize that the nonrational, gestalt-type experience that I have emphasized in this essay does not arise *ex nihilo*. Rather, such experience may be seen, in one respect at least, as often being the culmination of a process of conscious reflection.

This may be understood with particular clarity when we consider the revelatory role of the speculation about Jesus' role in salvation history that inevitably occurred among his disciples both during his lifetime and immediately after his death. On the one hand, the way I have suggested the full recognition of his significance came about—through a series of nonrational visionary experiences—suggests that such conscious speculation was effectively bypassed by unconscious processes. On the other hand, the way that those experiences manifested the assumptions of the prevailing culture may have been at least in part due to the content of that speculation. Indeed, as we have noted in relation to Rahner's thought, there are good theological reasons for seeing intellectual speculation, in the context of revelatory experience, as at least a component of the deeper, contemplative process that constitutes the foundation of that experience.

In relation to the Easter experiences, this general approach becomes highly suggestive when we remember that the expectation of resurrection had developed only relatively recently in the culture of Jesus' disciples. (D. S. Russell, for example, has noted that one of "the most remarkable developments during this period was the rise of a belief in life after death conceived in terms of resurrection.")[22] If one objects that the expectation was not of the resurrection of one man only but of all just people, and then only at the end of the age, this has no real significance when we remember not only that the end of the age was widely expected but also that the resurrection appearance accounts include the report that "many of God's people arose from sleep and, coming out of their graves after his resurrection, entered the holy city where many saw them" (Matt 27:53).

If this report is rightly to be rejected as indicating an empirical reality, it may, in the light of a psychological account of revelatory experience, still represent a true echo of the earliest experiences. One of the possible advantages of a visionary model of the Easter experiences is precisely that it puts into a new perspective some of the historical puzzles associated with the biblical accounts. The common assumption among commentators that certain biblical passages can have no historical basis because "things like that cannot happen" is challenged radically by a visionary model, in which the question of what might have been experienced historically does not coincide with what might have happened empirically.

An example that may be of particular interest is the account of Jesus' ascension in the Acts of the Apostles. Among almost all but fundamentalist commentators, this is judged to be a purely theological invention; the reasons are both well known and in the main rightly accepted.[23] Yet implicit in much of the argument is the notion that an ascension "event," which left those who experienced it "gazing intently into the sky" (Acts 1:10) can have no historical basis when the "place" of heaven is so clearly a culturally determined mistake. In terms of the culturally conditioned vision hypothesis, however, it seems quite possible that such an event could have been experienced. What can be experienced in visionary encounters depends not on what is objectively possible but on what is assumed possible in the prevailing culture. Indeed, when we take into account that the ascension motif had a particular prominence in the Judaism of the period,[24] it would almost be surprising if, in the context of a series of "resurrection" visions, there were not at least some manifestations in experience of the ascension theme.

These considerations may seem to some to have taken us a long way from an exploration of revelation as data. What they have been intended to convey, however, is precisely the complexity of attempting to combine a psychological understanding of revelatory experiences with a referential account of their content. Clearly, if we are to affirm what we might call *a psychological-referential model of revelatory experience,* then it will be necessary to do so in a carefully nuanced way. On the one hand, if revelatory experience is to be understood as referential (see chapter 4), then it is necessary to affirm the genuinely explanatory nature of the language that it evokes. On the other, considerations such as these mean that we must approach the question of theological language usage with a particularly open mind about the way it may be held to refer to the reality it describes.

7

The Puzzle-Solving Nature
of Theological Language Use

The question of theological language usage is, of course, not one that is limited to the type of consideration that we have examined so far. Indeed, it has been at the center of theological debate for many years, not least because of the widespread sense among theologians that the traditional framework of Christian theology requires radical modification. Keith Ward, for example, speaks for many when he says it is "clear that the Christian faith is a faith in crisis,"[1] and talks of the way in which the rise of the natural sciences, together with the growth of historical understanding and the acceptance of critical thinking, require that Christians pursue a new vision of how their faith should be expressed and a new understanding of how it can be seen as "truth."

Ward's own approach to this question has been interesting, however, in its unwillingness to set aside the belief that religious language may properly make certain fundamental truth claims. For while denying the validity of any one religious tradition's claim to exclusivism with respect to salvation, he also denies the validity of simply viewing all religious frameworks as equally true or false. Rather, he suggests that we need to adopt a "convergent pluralism," which "requires that most, and probably all, traditions will need to be revised to approximate more nearly to a fuller unitary truth which none of them yet fully encapsulates."[2]

The weakness of Ward's use of the concept of convergent pluralism lies, as we shall note further in chapter 11, less in its general framework—which has much to commend it—than in its lack of a focused concept of how relative truth in religious language is to be perceived. He rightly suggests, for example, that religion is "the pursuit of a vision. It is prompted by the trust that being is ultimately intelligible, morally demanding, and of supreme beauty. Such trust is founded upon disclosures of the ultimate character of being in various cultural and historical settings."[3] This insight is then expanded, however, in terms of a particular contrast of the language that arises from such a pursuit with that of science. Whereas, he asserts, "scientific thinking is largely about testing to destruction of hypotheses, religion is about the creative realization of a moral and transforming vision. . . . Whereas science is a matter of tentative hypotheses, religion is about being grasped by an overpowering ideal. Science offers predictive explanation, whereas religion pursues a goal that promises to integrate all life's endeavours. Science works by continued critical testing; religion by commitment to realize its ideal vision, by trust in the power which discloses it, shows the way to it and moves one towards it."[4]

This way of contrasting scientific and religious language is, as we have noted, not without a strong element of validity. As we have also pointed out, however, in recent years there has been a tendency to modify this type of contrast, albeit usually still with a foundationalist rather than a postfoundationalist mind-set.

Such work has tended to stress the similarities between the two types of language, causing the language of theology to be more widely perceived as exhibiting important parallels with that of science, at least at the level of methodology.[5] One aspect of this newer perspective, which as we have noted is related to aspects of Popper's work in the sciences, is that each type of language is seen as working with "models of reality" that are necessarily approximations subject to future modification. In this respect, at any rate, the newer approach seems compatible with Ward's convergent pluralism: it allows for future development of theological models of precisely the kind for which he pleads.

Supporters of this new emphasis on parallels between scientific and theological language use often, however, manifest a reliance on what is referred to as a "critical realism" about the entities and processes referred to in scientific and theological discussion. This notion of at least approximate reference to what exists in "reality" has still to be fully clarified, however. Indeed, as we shall see, even in the sciences the question of the ontological status of the entities referred to by theory continues to be hotly debated.[6] As a result, much of the work of theologians, in their exploration of the ramifications for theology of current understandings in the philosophy of science, has a somewhat provisional character.

Another way of approaching the possibility of parallels between the languages of science and theology has received little investigation, however, and it is this possibility I wish to pursue before tackling the question of realism. This alternative approach stands in agreement with much that has been said about the parallels between the two languages in recent debate, but maintains—at least initially—an agnostic attitude with regard to questions about ontology. This approach takes its bearings from the question of how the "puzzle solution" character of science—to use a phrase associated with Kuhn and with Larry Laudan[7]—may be applicable to theology. For this question can, it would seem, be explored independently of any particular assumptions about ontology. This possibility arises because the general agreement among philosophers of science about the method of puzzle-solving science coexists with a multiplicity of understandings of the ontological implications of scientists' puzzle-solving ability.

This general agreement is rooted in an understanding of scientists' "puzzle-solving" activity as essentially the application of a current theoretical framework to new areas of experience, in an attempt to seek understanding of that experience. Such activity is not, it is now widely agreed, simply the systemization of raw and arbitrarily chosen data. Rather, as we have noted, it involves the use of a current theoretical framework both to assess the significance of possible areas of experiment or observation and to understand the data arrived at in the chosen area. Whether they see the puzzle solving at the heart of this search for understanding as dealing with "increasing verisimilitude" and "real entities," or (as the antirealists would claim) merely with predictive success, few philosophers of science would now argue against the notion that puzzle-solving success is both the motivation and the justification of the scientific enterprise. (They recognize, too, that the majority of scientific practitioners, still with an essentially foundationalist-realist understanding of their discipline, might find this description inadequate to describe the source of their own motivation.)

At first sight, it would seem that this puzzle-solving character of the sciences has little or no parallel in theology. A cursory examination of the current state of theology would suggest that, at the descriptive level at any rate, any perceived parallel between science and theology breaks down at this point. For the entities of scientific theory—whatever one's judgment about their ontological status—are clearly embodied in theories or models that can be applied systematically over a wide range of phenomena. Indeed, choice of scientific theory is made possible (except, perhaps, in what Kuhn sees as a period of crisis heralding a new paradigm) precisely by what are perceived to be rational criteria for assessing the puzzle-solving ability of competing theories when applied to relevant data.[8]

Theological doctrine, by contrast, is often taken to be about unique "revelatory" phenomena, which by their nature are unrepeatable and not amenable to continuing observation or experiment. While the philosophically inclined theologian may perceive something of the puzzle-solving methodology in the traditional approach to certain theological "puzzles"—such as the existence of evil[9]—few Western theologians (with the partial exception, perhaps, of the incarnationists noted in chapter 3) would now find it possible to expound the purpose of theological doctrine in terms of a systematic exploration and understanding of the whole of human and cosmic experience. Rather, the conservative among them will tend to see doctrine simply as the systemization of certain events of "special revelation," differing from the nonconservative only in their certainty that a reliable account of those events is available.

As we have seen, there do exist postfoundationalist theologians such as J. Wentzel van Huyssteen who have challenged these simplistic approaches by acknowledging the complex rationality that must constitute the basis of good theological method. However, perhaps because of his belief that in a postfoundationalist theology "the focus will always, and first of all, be on a relentless criticism of uncritically held crypto-foundationalist assumptions,"[10] van Huyssteen himself has yet to explore that rationality in detail, and it remains the case that the current practice of the great majority of theologians in the West is such that any descriptive parallel between science and theology breaks down when the puzzle-solving element of the sciences is taken into account. The question remains, however, whether that element of scientific methodology might have any prescriptive value.

To talk of prescription based on scientific methodology does, of course, reek of the sort of "crypto-foundationalist assumptions" against which van Huyssteen has warned us. As he has said, "A postfoundationalist notion of rationality should . . . be able to open our epistemological eyes to broader and more complex notions of rationality, where scientific rationality—even if still our clearest example of cognitive rationality at work—cannot and should not be taken as normative for religious faith."[11] To ask whether an element of scientific methodology might have any prescriptive value for theology is not, however, to assume that such a prescription *must* be valid. Rather, as we have noted in the case of the concepts of coherence, scope, and fertility, it is simply to recognize that aspects of the rationality of scientific disciplines *may* turn out to be useful in a prescriptive sense. A rejection of the notion that theological rationality should be based on a foundationalist understanding of scientific rationality does not imply that scientific rationality, especially as now understood in a postfoundationalist context, has no characteristics from which theology can learn. On the contrary, as van Huyssteen has stressed, "in spite of important differences and sometimes radically different levels of explanation, theology and science do share common resources of rationality."[12] Whether the puzzle-solving character evident in scientific rationality is one of these common resources can only be decided based on detailed analysis.

One aspect of such an analysis should, I suggest, be the acknowledgment that a prescription for Christian theology in terms of a puzzle-solution approach would not always have appeared as eccentric as it often does today. Indeed, it can be argued that, historically, the emergence of a distinctively Christian theology was due almost entirely to the type of solution given to the "puzzle" posed by the character of Jesus and by the subsequent experience of the resurrection. The complexity of this puzzle for the early generations of his followers is witnessed to by the various christological trajectories that can be traced in the literature of the first and second centuries.

However, by examining the following centuries, during which much of the modern Christian conservative's vocabulary was coined and refined, we can make a better analysis of the puzzle-solving nature of Christian doctrine, since in this period methodological questions were less clouded by "data" problems caused by the widespread diffusion of what was later to be seen, almost universally, as apocryphal literature.[13] What becomes clear when we examine this later period is that the struggle for an acceptable theological language was never one merely of exegesis of the New Testament canon, which had by then been formed.

The actual development of doctrine in this period was, in fact, a complex process in which many criteria were implicitly at work. One that has perhaps been underestimated in recent analysis is the way that doctrine related to the "science" of the time—although largely in terms of an anagogical mode of interpretation[14] that would find few defenders today. It is not my purpose here to attempt such an analysis; I simply wish to note that the very complexity of the development of classical Christian doctrine points to the way that the debates—from which those doctrinal models emerged—involved questions of the implications of those models beyond the range of historical data from which they emerged.

A prime example is the way that the debates of the patristic era often revolved around the question of a proposed doctrine's soteriological implications.[15] The anti-Arian struggle in the fourth century, for example, had at least some of its roots in the concept of "theosis"—the idea that "God became man that man might become God." The explicit appeal to scripture to prove Christ's oneness of essence with the Father was always accompanied, at least implicitly, by an appeal to the "puzzle solutions" about human nature and vocation that the theory provided. Similarly, in the following centuries, the arguments about whether and how Christ could be said to have two natures and two wills, both human and divine, revolved around questions about what it was in human existence that Christ had assumed in order to heal.

In both cases, had it not been for the application of current theoretical models to matters other than what was accepted as the valid "revelatory" data from which they had arisen, it is doubtful whether the problems of doctrinal definition would have evolved as they did. As it was, the advent of an effectively "new" theoretical problem— the soteriological one—demanded an evolution of christological theory that made certain previously acceptable manifestations of that theory seem inadequate. Over and over in the early centuries, the soteriological puzzle solutions offered by competing models were an influential factor in the formation of doctrine whenever appeal to the "raw data" of revelation seemed ambiguous.

The criteria by which such judgments were made would not necessarily appeal to the modern theologian, any more than the judgments of scientists of earlier centuries would appear adequate to their scientific successors today. Still, in patristic theology, evolution toward what was seen as a wider comprehensiveness and accuracy followed a path similar to that of modern science, with new models replacing or extending old ones through criteria that went beyond mere systematizing of data whose authenticity was accepted. Even when the "scriptural" data itself was agreed on, different theoretical models arose. Model choice depended at least partly on a further question: Which of the competing models is consonant with the spiritual and empirical experience that the Christian has of his or her existence and redemption?

It is for this historical reason that assertions of the need to abandon traditional theological doctrines are often simplistic. It is not adequate simply to comment "If I ask 'How do I know Jesus is God?' I only have the gospels as evidence. But if the Gospel beliefs are sometimes false; if in fact their whole picture of the world . . . is false, or at best alien to our own way of seeing the world, the evidence looks rather shaky."[16] In fact, the church's doctrine of the incarnation, while relying in part on what we would now regard as shaky or even incredible historical evidence, was not only grounded in the supposed historical reliability of such evidence, nor was it simply a systematizing of that evidence. Rather, it reflected, as has always been the case in religious language, an important existential dimension.

This way of looking at the development of doctrine does not imply a straightforward existentialist framework for patristic thought, but such historical considerations do point to an area of contact between the modern theology influenced by existentialism and that which became definitive for the church in the patristic era—an area of contact that has not been lost on at least one school of neopatristic theology at the present time. The most direct heirs of the patristic writers, who have developed this implicit understanding of theological language use, have continued to utilize an inherited language in a way that has preserved this insight into its applicability. Within the framework of Eastern Orthodoxy, that most patristic of contemporary traditions, not only have the soteriological insights that informed the patristic consensus remained potent, but theologians such as Christos Yannaras[17] and John Zizioulas[18] have, quite independently of any scientific criteria of the sort explored here, made explicit this "puzzle-solution" aspect of patristic theology in a fascinating way.

Each, in a way that combines powerful loyalty to the patristic tradition with insights from Western existentialism, has extended the view of what it is to be human developed by Orthodox writers of an earlier generation—a theological anthropology, as Vladimir Lossky put it, "constructed from the top down, beginning from Trinitarian and Christological dogma."[19] What is meant by this stress on a "top downwards" methodology is that the starting point for a theological anthropology is not the "raw data" of the empirical human condition, but rather the "revealed data" of the nature of the God in whose image and likeness human beings are made and redeemed. One example is the way these writers see the doctrine of the Trinity as having crucial implications for a proper understanding of humanity in terms of interrelatedness and interdependence between human persons—an approach not unknown in the West,[20] but rarely based upon so explicit a theological methodology.

In constructing their anthropology in this way, such writers are doing something that has strong parallels in scientific methodology. For just as the scientist does not simply start with random raw data, but chooses what seems to be significant from the point of view of his or her current framework and then seeks to understand the data within that framework, so such writers are similarly going about their task. Just as the modern physicist will, methodologically, take it for granted that, say, the basic theory of general relativity will be applicable to the motion of bodies under all circumstances, and will choose areas of research and seek an understanding of the results in the context of that theory, so the theologian of this school will approach the task of theology with a similar confidence in both the basic theory of his discipline and in the "top downwards" mode of its applicability.

Such a "top downwards" application of a doctrinal framework seems highly suspect to a Western generation whose theological focus has been on how the doctrinal frameworks themselves have evolved historically from the experiences that lay behind them. Those critical of that evolution have essentially called for a new working from the bottom upwards, and much effort has gone into the questions of what "revelatory" data can be considered reliable and what might be inferred from it in a theory-independent way. From the point of view of a prescriptive theological method derived from the sciences, however, this historical focus of modern Western theology, though far from irrelevant, tends to miss the point of what constitutes true puzzle-solving activity. Such activity by its very nature is, as we have noted, always a top-downwards activity, in which theoretical models are permitted to define what makes for relevant data and how that data may be treated.[21]

An important characteristic of such a methodology—one particularly evident in the modern Eastern Orthodox approach—inevitably raises questions for the modern Western theologian. This is the element of "fundamentalism" inherent in the application of any given theory in a "top-downward" methodology. For those involved in the present theological "crisis" in the Christian West—those for whom even the basic doctrinal formulae of traditional Christianity are now suspect—there is the suspicion that an approach that manifests such calm confidence in the validity of these formulae can hardly be taken seriously. For even the mildly radical, such conservatism seems to have no role in theological development.

This suspicion is challenged, however, by an understanding of the role of conservatism in scientific development. Periods of crisis like the present one in theology are familiar to historians and philosophers of science. The breakdown of classical Newtonian mechanics and its replacement by a relativistic successor, for example, has provided a key example for those studying periods of crisis in the evolution of scientific thought. For Kuhn, in particular, such periods stand in important contrast to those long periods of "normal" science, in which there is a general "assurance that the old paradigm will solve all its problems, that nature can be shoved into the box the paradigm provides."[22] Only after prolonged mismatch between theory and data, he suggests, will such assurance in the scientific community begin to crumble. He sees the crisis brought on by this crumbling as important in its loosening of the normal rules of scientific work and the concomitant possibility of a revolutionary leap in understanding. Conservatives and radicals then, in his analysis, exist side by side until either the old framework is seen to solve the problems that have arisen or else a revolutionary leap of understanding arises from the radical side.

We have already related how the Eastern Orthodox theologians cited above apply doctrinal theory with the calm confidence of the physicist applying the basic equations of general relativity. In essence, such theologians are working in a way that parallels the work of all scientists in an era of normal science, or of conservative scientists in a time of crisis. However, many of the theologians involved in the current Western theological crisis are not behaving in the way that they would if their discipline were truly a puzzle-solving one. While the conservatives retreat into either ecclesial or scriptural "tradition," and see the inherited doctrinal framework simply as an expression of the given data of special revelation, the more radical often tend to see the problem as essentially historical, and simply abandon the inherited framework, accepting the conservatives' estimate of its status and seeing it as irrelevant to the resolution of the crisis.

By contrast, radical scientists, when in a similar position, though they may begin to lose faith and to consider alternatives, do not renounce the theoretical framework that has led them into crisis. Rather (and here most of Kuhn's opponents agree with his general thesis, if not with some of its details and emphases), it is precisely the conservatism of scientists—their reluctance to abandon inherited and in many ways still useful frameworks—that makes both normal or puzzle-solving science possible and leads, when necessary, to revolutionary change. For it is only through such normal science that the professional community of scientists succeeds, first, in exploiting the potential scope and precision of the older framework and, then, in isolating the difficulty through the study of which a new one may emerge.

Thus, if theology is to be a successful puzzle-solving activity, it would seem, ironically, that this might require that conservatism be one of its characteristics, and not least when revolutionary change becomes necessary. Such conservatism means not merely adherence to certain basic tenets when applied to a limited range of phenomena, but a willingness to explore their applicability well beyond that range; it is here that many Western theologians, conservative and radical alike, seem to have abandoned the methodology prescribed by scientific practice.

If theologians are to accept this prescription, however, it is important to recognize that while the general concept of a puzzle-solving activity can be articulated most clearly through an examination of scientific methodology, the type of puzzle solution to be sought in theology is distinctive. The examples of theological puzzle-solving methodology that I have used—those of patristic and modern Eastern Orthodox theologians—indicate clearly the way that the level of complexity with which theology deals has often evoked a rationality, distinctive in this respect. The use of these examples does not, however, necessarily indicate that a puzzle-solving methodology for theology is limited to such issues. Indeed, in a contemporary context the main questions that are illuminated by a puzzle-solving prescription for theology are perhaps precisely those with which we have been dealing throughout this essay: those arising from the modern dialogue of science and theology. It is, therefore, back to these that we must now turn.

8

Puzzle Solutions
and the Theology of Nature

In addition to the pansacramentalist naturalism that I have advocated, a number of approaches exist that see fields of reference of science and theology as overlapping or interpenetrating, albeit with the sciences having an autonomy in their own field of applicability.[1] In the context of a discussion of theology's puzzle-solving nature, two of these are of particular interest because, through their attempts to formulate a theology of nature, they not only seek to examine this interpenetration of theology and the natural sciences, but also to illustrate the two main ways in which theology and the sciences may be held to interact.

The first of these, associated primarily with the name of Thomas Torrance, has arisen, as we have seen, from an essentially "Barthian" theological framework. Natural theology, in this view, must be developed in terms of its "inner correlation" with revealed theology, analogous to the correlation geometry has with physics. As such, according to Torrance, it will remain simply "the pliant conceptual instrument which theology uses in unfolding and expressing the content of real knowledge of God."[2] This inner correlation does, it would seem, provide a sufficient link between the natural world and God's revelatory acts for a puzzle-solution methodology to be appropriate; indeed, the sort of puzzle-solution approach that, as we have seen, is characteristic of the patristic and Eastern Orthodox traditions, seems to be a natural corollary of Torrance's approach. It is therefore no surprise to find that his doctrinal sympathies with these traditions are considerable.[3]

The difficulty with such a view, from the perspective of an exploration of a puzzle-solving methodology, lies not in a lack of relationship between natural phenomena and revelatory action, but in its inability to provide any sort of radical critique. Torrance's approach has been so colored by the Barthian framework's stress on the transcendent otherness of God that the "natural theology" that it allows—a "pliant conceptual instrument"—is severely restricted in scope. It is, in fact, so pliant that it is not robust enough for tasks other than essentially apologetic or weakly explanatory ones. It simply fails to allow awkward "puzzles" inherent in experience to affect the basic framework of theology. The appearance of an apparently insoluble puzzle is simply due, it is assumed, to an inadequate grasp of God's self-disclosure in acts of special revelation.

For this reason, it is a second way of viewing the inner correlation between a theology of nature and "revealed" theology, which is in practice more fruitful, in that it does allow a real and critical exploration of the latter. This approach is based on the strong sense of divine immanence to be found in the earlier works of Arthur Peacocke and of John Polkinghorne, which we examined briefly in chapter 1. This approach, like Torrance's, also stresses that acts of special revelation are not arbitrary in relation to the world's process. In this approach, however, the continuity between God's continuous action and his "special" revelatory action is stressed in such a way that, even from a supernaturalist standpoint, each is allowed to illuminate the other in our understanding.

Polkinghorne, for example, while firmly refusing any account of God's relation to the cosmos that in any way compromises the concept of his transcendence and omnipotence, equally firmly insists that God, as the one who is faithful, "must show reliability in his relationship with his world. He will not be an arbitrary intervener in its processes, but they will have about them a consistency which reflects his character."[4] This leads him to the further denial "that one can satisfactorily speak about the doctrine of creation without taking into account the actual nature of the world."[5] Though working it out in an essentially conservative way, he echoes the concerns of other scientifically trained theologians, for whom, in the words of Arthur Peacocke, "various features of the scientific landscape modify and enlarge . . . the way we may conceive God's relation to the world."[6] In such a view, the cosmos, created by God *ex nihilo* as the appropriate setting for his providential and salvific actions, in itself says something about its creator. Although this cannot be fully articulated without taking into account the events of "special" revelation, which make the meaning of God's continuous action intelligible, those "unique" events, as special cases of the way that God acts continuously in the world, can be comprehended only partially unless seen in proper relation to that continuous activity.

As we have seen, there are problems with Polkinghorne's own view of how this should be done. The important thing, however, is that (at least in his earlier work) he, like Peacocke, has assumed that a proper theology of nature and a theology rooted in revelation are to be linked by a sort of iterative procedure in which there is no dualism between the "nature" explored in the one and the "grace" explored in the other. It was precisely an extrapolation from this general approach that led to the psychological model of revelatory experience that we explored in chapter 3. What is important here, however, is quite independent of that model. The type of theology of nature for which people like Polkinghorne and Peacocke make claims has far greater potential for theological development, in terms of puzzle-solving ability, not only than Torrance's approach but also than either the patristic emphasis on soteriology or the theological anthropology of the Eastern Orthodox, which we have noted.

The latter, though highly suggestive, have the problem that they refer not directly to the empirical human condition, but rather to the redeemed humanity of the "new creation," which is related to the empirical scene largely through "spiritual experience," ethics, and ecclesiology. As such, they throw up challenges and allow refinement of doctrine only indirectly. In this sense, the patristic and modern Orthodox approaches conform to the scientific parallel only insofar as that parallel is interpreted in terms of seeking understanding in a narrow sense. Rather than seeking understanding in a way that is open to a genuine challenge to their basic theological frameworks, the tendency of these approaches is to impose models rather than allow them to develop in a way that might bring to light the need for radical modification.

What is needed for such a challenge is the identification of areas of experience in which theological "prediction" is open to real difficulty, and it is precisely here that the theology of nature that we have noted is of crucial importance. The scientifically perceived realities of creation, in their highly evolved contemporary state, inevitably challenge the picture of their creator as received through an inherited framework of thought with its roots in "special" revelation. The task of developing the Christian's inherited theological framework to make it consonant with the modern scientific perception of the processes at work in the world is, as a result, one of the most exciting and exacting tasks of contemporary theology.

It may be, of course, that the present widespread focus on the natural sciences will be but a first step in this task, because one of the main challenges to traditional theology comes not from the natural but from the human sciences—chiefly, perhaps, in the area of human psychology,[7] and not least, in the way that I have outlined, in its relation to fundamental religious experience. Until now, however, such challenges have provided few constructive clues to the development of Christian doctrine, whereas the natural sciences provide a number of examples that illuminate the way a puzzle-solving methodology might allow theology to enter into a fuller dialogue with the human sciences.

One such example is the question of how the scientifically perceived roles of law and chance in the natural world affect the concept of God's action in the world. This constitutes, as Jacques Monod stresses from an atheist's perspective,[8] a crucial theological puzzle. From the theological perspective, however, it is precisely the type of puzzle that is fruitful according to the method I have outlined, offering a real challenge to the basis of any theological framework. The responses of the scientist-apologists, only some of which we have noted, have already been sufficiently wide-ranging to make it clear that, as Arthur Peacocke has put it, "at last, theology has a chance to respond to questions which are actually being asked in the context of our present scientific culture. In responding . . . theology will find that there is scarcely any one of the 'heads' of Christian doctrine, as they used to be called, that is not affected by the new perspective. Perhaps one day a new coherent theology might emerge prompted by this stimulus and so continue in our own day what, for example, the Cappadocian Fathers and St. Thomas Aquinas did in their times in relation to contemporary philosophy and science."[9]

For such a coherent theology to be possible, however, the implicit methodology adopted thus far by those responding to scientific developments requires clarification and articulation. It is here, it would seem, that the sort of puzzle-solving methodology for theology that I have outlined has its most important immediate application, as it may help to illuminate a methodology already implicit in such work.

An example of such a methodological question is: When can a doctrinal change proposed in the course of puzzle-solving activity be held to be valid? In the dialogue of science and theology, as we have already noted, this question arises in a number of areas, and the need for such criteria will become even more essential with the advent of proposals for more major doctrinal change, of the kind implicit in the arguments of the earlier sections of this essay, and which we shall examine in more detail in chapter 11. It is of importance, therefore, to recognize that such criteria arise naturally in a puzzle-solving methodology, because criteria for theory change in the latter are already well articulated in relation to the natural sciences. It may well be, of course, that these criteria will need to be expanded in order to be applicable to theology; nevertheless, their general outline can only be helpful toward that expansion.

Put simply, the abandonment of an existing theory T1 for another, T2, requires, in the sciences, that certain conditions be fulfilled. In pre-Kuhnian terms, this could be stated as the condition that T2 should subsume T1: that it had to work as well as its predecessor in areas in which that predecessor was "successful," and either exclude an aspect of it that was erroneous in those areas, or else be applicable to a wider range of phenomena. Kuhn himself emphasized that when the statement is applied to a wide theoretical framework—what he called a paradigm—things might not be quite this simple. Nevertheless, he suggested that a candidate for a new paradigm, to be successful, must "solve some outstanding and generally recognized problem that can be met in no other way ... [and] promise to preserve a relatively large part of the problem-solving ability that had accrued to science through its predecessors."[10]

Applied to theology, such criteria, together with Kuhn's affirmation of the reluctance to abandon existing theory until such criteria are met, would seem to have two major implications. First, any candidate for a new theory or, more radically, for a new conceptual and methodological framework, must promise to do at least as much, by way of puzzle-solving, as could the old. There may be—as in the sciences in the Kuhnian analysis—a problem of "incommensurability" in which competing schools cannot entirely agree on what the new candidate promises to do and what constitutes "valid past achievement." Proponents of the new, even if they cannot persuade their opponents to agree with their judgment, must be clear that what they propose really is more comprehensive in scope than what they seek to replace or at least potentially as comprehensive, while also being in some respect more accurate.

The second implication of this insight from the sciences is that what a physicist might call a "correspondence principle" will connect the old theory to any new one that has validly replaced it. According to this principle, the old theory will still give the right "result" over a certain range of circumstances; where it is easier to use within that range, such use is legitimate. (Thus, for example, no physicist will use Einstein's relativistic equations in those circumstances—easily defined—in which Newton's "less correct" but more easily manipulable ones will give the same result.) Applied to theology, such a principle suggests that there may be some areas of experience for which the traditional language of Christian theology and worship will still provide an adequate "explanation," and that where this is simpler to use than that which has replaced it, such use will be legitimate. In this, there is a strong conservative element in a puzzle-solving theology, as in the sciences.

An example of a proposed change that seems to meet both these criteria is, I would suggest, that which is implicit in Arthur Peacocke's sacramental panentheism, which we noted in chapter 2. On the one hand, there is the potential for fundamental doctrinal change, insofar as, for example, Peacocke's system allows, as we have noted, a fundamental reinterpretation of the doctrine of the incarnation. This does, arguably, promise a greater explanatory power than does the traditional doctrine, in that creation and incarnation can be seen as aspects of a single act, by comparison with which the traditional understanding seems somewhat arbitrary. At the same time, all that the original doctrine of the incarnation could be said to have achieved—a way of talking about Jesus as the culminative act of creation and redemption—is retained. Indeed, in terms of each of Barbour's categories of agreement with data, coherence, scope, and fertility, noted previously, an evolutionary Christology such as Peacocke's seems to have much to commend it.[11]

The historical background to this possibility is illuminating here, because Peacocke's thinking in this respect seems to have its roots in that particular Anglican tradition, which, as he has noted, involves a "stress on the doctrine of the Incarnation, and on a sacramental understanding of the world with its concomitant emphasis on the sacraments of the church."[12] The understanding of the sacramental nature of the natural world to which this emphasis gave rise, however, seems at some stage to have become for him the prime doctrinal belief from which all else flows—including Christ's own "incarnation." This development, it should be noted, became possible not because the person of Jesus ceased to be central to Peacocke's thinking. Rather, it seems that he formulated a way of beginning not with a doctrinal expression of that significance but with the existential *fact* of it, which he was able to interpret in a way which took into account both the belief in divine action that he has as a result of that existential fact and the knowledge of the world that he has as a scientist. His continuing use of "incarnation" language is, therefore, not in the least inappropriate in relation to the Christian understanding of the person of Jesus, and provides an excellent example of the sort of correspondence principle continuity of language that we have noted.

Moreover, Peacocke's proposed change in understanding the incarnation in no way affects the conclusions of the sort of "incarnationism" that we examined in chapter 3. Nothing that is seen by incarnationists as flowing from the doctrine of the incarnation is lost in the sacramental panentheism of Peacocke's approach. Thus, it would be quite proper, within that approach, to maintain the language of incarnation in relation to those aspects of the world that an older incarnationism explores. In the framework of sacramental panentheism, the incarnation need not be seen as the act from which an incarnationist analysis flows, but rather as a provisional doctrinal formulation of a particular (and for the Christian, historically foundational) example of the type of divine action to which sacramental panentheism points. In other words, incarnationism, as a broad understanding, need not depend on the traditional doctrine of the incarnation, but may be seen as a more fundamental theological insight into the way that God acts generally in the world.

Comparison of the evolution of theological doctrine with that of scientific theory suggests, however, that the continuity of "incarnationist" language that Peacocke's development of a sacramental panentheism allows will not necessarily always be possible in fundamental doctrinal change. If scientific theory occasionally goes through revolutions in the Kuhnian sense, so also, we might guess, could theological doctrine. In relation to the development of a theology of the world's faiths, for example, it would hardly be surprising if at least some of the traditional categories of Christian doctrine were to prove inapplicable according to the correspondence principle.

Here, therefore, the wider criteria for doctrinal change inherent in the puzzle-solving methodology may well have their part to play.

Indeed, these wider criteria will constitute a framework that is lacking in an analysis such as Ward's. There is much to be said, for example, for his general comments that all religious traditions "need to pass through the critical crisis" so that by "a process of dialectical interpenetration, in which understanding can develop within each tradition, they may converge on a more adequate understanding of the ultimate goal. The tests of authenticity will be of moral sensitivity, experiential depth and capacity to effect personal integration, as well as upon coherence with other well-attested knowledge, internal consistency, capacity to suggest a highly-integrated world-view and fruitfulness in suggesting further quests for understanding."[13] The more existential of these criteria are, however, as Ian Barbour has noted of such criteria generally, "unescapably ambiguous and reflect the norms of one's own traditions."[14] Ultimately, therefore, while existential questions must remain integral to the internal development of any one tradition, only the sort of paradigm-challenging question that we have noted will allow a degree of genuine (if inevitably still only partial) commensurability in dialogue between religious traditions.

The arguments of this chapter and of the last have been somewhat complex; therefore, it may be helpful here to recapitulate. My argument has been that a methodological prescription for theology, derived largely from a postfoundationalist model of the successful activity of the natural sciences, is one that can provide general criteria for the development of theological language, applicable to any new development or restatement of an old position within the subject. I have suggested that such criteria point to a new appreciation of the existential dimension of the patristic synthesis as an important element in the internal development of Christian doctrine, and that a potentially more radical element in that development arises from attempts to develop a theology of the world's faiths and from the dialogue between theology and both the natural and human sciences. The latter, in particular, I have suggested, may prove to be the crucial arena in which the future of Christian doctrine is worked out.

These criteria for development and even revolution in doctrine, however, imply for the Christian an essentially conservative rooting in what have traditionally been described as the revelatory and saving acts of God in Christ. Such a theology will enter into a puzzle-solving dialogue with secular disciplines in which no artic-ulation of that traditional starting point is sacrosanct. Neverthe-less, as we have seen, this potentially revolutionary framework involves a "top-downward" methodology, which at first sight may seem conservative or even fundamentalist, while other conserva-tive features arise from the associated criteria for valid doctrinal change.

Such conclusions, I have stressed, are compatible with a post-foundationalist understanding of human rationality and, while compatible with them, do not rely either on a psychological under-standing of revelation or on any particular understanding of the mode of reference to—or the ontology of—the entities and rela-tionships of which traditional Christian theology speaks. For just as in the sciences there are several understandings of the ontological issue within a broad consensus about the sciences' puzzle-solving nature, so there could be in theology. My prescription of a method-ology for theology, derived from the puzzle-solving nature of scien-tific enquiry, is therefore not inherently untenable from the point of view of any particular theory of theological reference, and could be adopted by both instrumentalists and critical realists alike. Its appli-cation to the questions about revelation and reference with which we began our considerations of theological language, requires, however, an interpretation that assumes at least some kind of realism. It is therefore to the question of realism in theological language that we must now turn.

9

Structure not Substance:
A Radically Modified Realism

Many of those who have developed arguments for a putative realism in theology[1] have done so on the basis of parallels between theological and scientific language usage that, as we have noted, have excited much comment in recent years. Their conclusion has been that theological models may be seen as having essentially the same function and status as scientific ones, interpreted in terms of a realism that is "critical" in the sense of acknowledging, in a Popperian way, that current theories and their ontologies are susceptible to future modification. Most of those who have undertaken to defend theological realism in this way have, however, written as if unaware of what Alister McGrath has rightly called "a widespread perception that a non-foundationalist epistemology requires a nonrealist metaphysics."[2] They have not therefore even attempted to assert, as McGrath has, that this perception "is quite unwarranted."[3]

Nor, on the whole, have these defenders of theological realism manifested a full appreciation of the nuances of the debate about realism in the philosophy of science. They often fail, for example, to recognize the way that purely historical considerations point toward the problematic nature of the ontology attributed to scientific models. As antirealists are always quick to point out, not only do the apparent ontological claims of scientific theories change with time, but there is sometimes also a lack of any coherent direction in successive changes. Kuhn rightly observes, for example, that while "Newton's mechanics improves on Aristotle's and . . . Einstein's improves on Newton's as instruments for puzzle-solving," these successive theories manifest "no coherent direction in their ontological development. On the contrary, in some important respects, though by no means in all, Einstein's general theory of relativity is closer to Aristotle's than either of them is to Newton's."[4]

This historical problem is, moreover, simply one aspect of a more general philosophical problem with which the scientific realist must grapple: that of the connection between the success of a theory and its truth or approximate truth. If present theories are likely to be replaced at some future time with other theories with different ontological descriptions, how can we assess the success of the current ontology? To speak, as some do, of a realism in relation to entities rather than theories is to sidestep rather than to answer adequately the question of what it means to say that the entities posited by current theory are "something like" those that actually exist. If the realist talks in terms of Popperian "increasing verisimilitude," the antirealist can respond persuasively in terms of the apparent impossibility either of quantifying this increase or of specifying the aspects of the theory to which it applies. Indeed, the realist can say that arguments for realism have often manifested a surprising lack of philosophical rigor,[5] and in practice the problems associated with the realist position have not been solved, "even to the satisfaction of realists."[6]

Thus, when Ian Barbour characterizes a critical realism in relation to the entities of scientific theory in terms of the way in which scientific models "make tentative ontological claims that there are entities in the world something like those postulated in the models,"[7] he fails to do justice to the way in which, as Jarrett Leplin has put it, such a realism constitutes "a majority position whose advocates are so divided as to appear a minority."[8] In particular, precisely the type of "tentative ontological claims" made by a realist approach has been left so vague by Barbour and others that the crucial question of precisely what a critically realist understanding implies for the ontology of doctrinal statements is left largely unanswered in their analyses. It would seem, therefore, that there has been something rather premature in much of the theological work that has argued from a rather general understanding of realism in the sciences to a putative parallel realism in theology. Nancey Murphy, among others, has been right to urge caution in view of the way in which even scientific realism is "a problematic position philosophically."[9]

This does not mean, however, that none of the approaches so far has been fruitful. In particular, in the work of Janet Soskice[10] (whose arguments have been taken up in an accessible way by Arthur Peacocke[11]), the argument for theological and scientific realism has been started in a convincing way by considering much wider questions of language usage and reference. This approach adopts the theory of reference associated with the names of Hilary Putnam, Saul Kripke, and Keith Donellan,[12] which tackles the problem of revised description in theory change by emphasizing that continuity of reference is not necessarily negated by such revision.

In reaction to those theories that assume the meaning of a term is specified by a conjunction of properties, these authors have pointed in their different ways to a "causal" concept of reference. They point to the way that proper names, together with the names of what they call "natural kinds," may at different times be described in terms of different properties and yet still manifest continuity of reference. Reference is in fact determined, they suggest, by an initial "dubbing event," in which some object or sample is given a name. At this stage, knowledge of the actual properties of the thing dubbed may be minimal, and may only be discovered gradually as the community, handing on the name from person to person in a causal chain, investigates the thing dubbed.

Thus, for example, water may have initially been dubbed as such and then its reference (in the language of Kripke) "fixed" in terms of a series of properties of the substance—its liquid nature, colorlessness, and so on. However, it is possible that some other substance may have exactly these fixing properties and yet not, chemically, be water. It is also logically possible for a substance to be water, chemically, and yet not to satisfy the list of properties that fixed the reference. Proponents of this theory of reference hold that the substance, water, has its reference defined not by the conjunction of properties that fixed it following the dubbing event, but by its real essence—in this case, its chemical composition, H_2O. They assert that even if, in the process of the investigation of water up to the discovery of its chemical composition, there had been changes in the list of properties that were held to be characteristic of it, this would not mean that different things had been referred to at different stages of the investigation.

Such a theory of reference has been attractive to theologians, because it not only seems to allow for a realist theology that may nevertheless progress from one doctrinal framework to another, but it also stresses the role of the community, which a Christian theologian can easily interpret in terms of the importance of the church as the body of Christ. The very attractiveness of these features means, however, that some of the philosophical problems of reference to things other than samples (or people, on which the theory has also focused) are perhaps underestimated in their appropriation of this approach.

Such problems are, however, instructive, and arguably point to a fuller and more persuasive development of the realist position. Rom Harré, for example, in his account of what he calls referential realism, has explored the question of reference outside of these categories by making a distinction between what, following the work of L. Roberts, he calls DC and IP reference modes. The former is that on which the standard account is based, involving the use of a demonstrative (D) and a complement (C) as, for example, in the statement, "This gray powder is a sample of gallium." Such a statement requires simply the ability, as he puts it, "to pick out a figure from a ground." An IP attribution, by contrast, involves an indefinite pronoun (I) and an individuating predicate (P) as, for example, in the statement "Whatever is the cause of these bubbles is a neutrino." Here, we have not only what Harré calls the "material practice" of picking out a figure from a ground, but also the cognitive act of conceiving and accepting a theoretical account of the possible causes of strings of bubbles.[13]

The importance of this distinction is that in the sciences the IP mode of reference, which Harré takes as genuinely referential, is almost always uncritically translated into the DC mode through an ontological assumption that has nothing to do with the mode of reference concerned. As an example, he notes that there is nothing in the IP description of the neutrino that makes it necessary to conceive it as it is usually conceived: as a particle. Indeed, he notes, an alternative metaphysics to that of particles is available through David Bohm's work on the "implicate order."[14] Nevertheless, he says, the present overwhelming influence of corpuscular concepts makes it natural to read the IP format for the neutrino in a particulate DC mode, so that it becomes: "Whatever is the cause of momentum disparity in beta decay is a particle of zero rest mass and no charge moving in such and such a trajectory." He goes on, "Only if taken referentially does this statement license the undertaking of a spatio-temporal search for traces of the passage of a being of a kind defined by these parameters. But there is nothing in the IP format itself that would require that its referents be conceived as particulate. The logical grammar of the . . . IP referential format is neutral. It is the conservative metaphysical predilections of physicists that push the ontology that way."[15]

A similar recognition of a metaphysical interpretative act in assigning an ontology to a theoretical description is to be found in the recent work of Mary Hesse. She argues that while scientific progress can properly be interpreted in realist terms, this does not mean that one can defend the "substantial realism" implicit in many accounts of critical realism. This latter she defines as "the view that successful theoretical ontologies, or models, not only approximately describe real nature, but describe it increasingly accurately as one theory succeeds another in a sort of limiting process towards the truth."[16] By contrast, she herself believes, like Kuhn, that while there is genuine and continuous increase in what Kuhn would call the sciences' puzzle-solving ability, there is no coherent direction of ontological development that necessarily accompanies this.

Unlike Kuhn, however, Hesse does not believe that this necessarily leads to an antirealist interpretation. Rather, she develops a form of realism not unlike Harré's, which she calls a "structural realism," defined by a number of theses, the first three of which are:

1. Physics presupposes that natural objects have properties and relations that can be specified with ever-increasing accuracy.
2. Objects are related by causal laws in an all-embracing network which can be specified with ever-increasing accuracy and universality.
3. These presuppositions have been notably successful in building up comparatively simple, unified theories which permit accurate application, extrapolation and prediction, and these predictions are remarkably well confirmed by experiment. It follows that the mathematical programme for "world construction" captures such reality of the world as permits this application to be successful. This is the core of structural realism.[17]

It is, Hesse says, "undeniable that mathematical structures become ever more unified and universal with every advance in theory; the structural realm of physics is truly progressive. But the substantial description of what the structures relate changes radically from theory to theory."[18] This can happen, she thinks, because of the nature of the *interpretation* of those mathematical relationships of which the laws of physics consist. Such interpretation is necessary to connect the mathematical structure with empirical observation and experiment. In this sense, it is intrinsic to the physicist's understanding; without it, that understanding could be neither developed nor applied. Nevertheless, she asserts, such interpretation is, as far as questions about realism are concerned, secondary. As a picture of the ontology of the world, it is unreliable in the sense of being susceptible—unlike the mathematical relationships themselves—to complete change or abandonment.

What these approaches of Harré and Hesse suggest, in different ways, is that while antirealist interpretations of science are untenable, a coherent scientific realism should not be seen in terms of the substantial, ontological interpretation of the entities described by scientific theories, which inevitably has a metaphysical component that might change drastically in the future course of theory development. In some sense, they suggest, the entities with which theories populate the world do not have the characteristics of the relational categories of those theories that properly permit a realist understanding. A realism of this sort suggests, in fact, that relational terms are more fundamental and reliable than ones used to describe the entities thus related, essential as the latter may be as heuristic devices.

Scientific critical realism is, then, when viewed from this sort of perspective, something rather more subtle and complex than it often appears in theological apologetic, which claims a similar realism for religious language. This is not to say, however, that the arguments for such a critical realism in theology are thereby rendered redundant. Rather, if we find those arguments compelling or even suggestive, then what becomes necessary is an examination of the way in which a structural realism, of the Hesse variety, might affect the way a putatively realistic theological language should be used and understood.

10

Structural Realism
and the Language of Theology

In considering the implications for theology of a structural realism as examined in the last chapter, perhaps we should first note that such a realism has not been absent from analyses of critical realism in theology, although it has been rather unfocused. Arthur Peacocke, for example, in discussing the role of models in science and theology, points out that such models "are concerned less with picturing objects than with depicting processes, relations and structures (i.e., patterns of relationship.) What matter is 'in itself' and what God is 'in himself' are left as unknown and unknowable."[1] Similarly Janet Soskice, in her defense of metaphorical theological language, makes explicit use of causal theories of reference, using a concept of the "dubbing event" that can be seen as equivalent to the IP mode analyzed by Harré. In relation to the language used to describe mystical experience, for example, she says, "there is no reason why the mystics' claims, although qualified and couched in the language of their particular mystical tradition, should not be referential. The essential claim, the 'dubbing event', is something like 'Whatever caused this experience is God.'"[2]

What Soskice leaves only partially explored, however, is the way (to use terms other than those that she herself adopts) the IP reference mode of such a statement is inevitably translated, at least implicitly, into a DC statement. A mystic belonging to a culture rooted in the Judeo-Christian-Islamic tradition, for example, will, when saying, "Whatever caused this experience is God," be doing far more than making a referential statement in an IP format. "God," for those in this tradition, is not merely an IP labeling word. Their very use of the word will at least implicitly involve a translation into a DC format—through the use of metaphysical assumptions about divine personhood, for example, which Buddhists, in a comparable situation, simply would not make.[3]

This is not to say that Soskice fails to recognize the way in which terms used in referential statements are theory-laden. However, while rightly arguing that "the referential value of the claim is not . . . affected by being articulated in theory-laden terms," she tends to see this value in terms of a somewhat simplistic concept of the possibility of error. "To show that the use of [such] terms refers," she says, "does not guarantee that these are experiences . . . of the Christian God, or of any god at all; but this is only to say that realism involves the possibility of error."[4] While this is true, however, a recognition of the distinction between substantial realism and structural realism provides a far more nuanced understanding of where that error might lie. It is not merely a matter of whether or not, in the words of Soskice, "the mystics and those following them may be sadly misguided as to the cause of their experience."[5] It is a matter also—as we have seen—of the extent to which an arbitrary metaphysical interpretative scheme has been seen as intrinsic to the referential statements.

An example of the way such schemes have had their effect in the past is provided by the Christian use of the classical credal statement that Jesus Christ is of one *ousia* with God the Father. For the "sub-stantia" or "substance" of the commonest Latin and English translations of this term in the Nicene Creed has often been understood in static, quasi-Aristotelian terms. Though the best trinitarian thought of modern times avoids any such understanding, as did the patristic theology through which the term was moulded, it is easy to see why some believe, with John Hick: "The main feature of the Nicene and Chalcedonian formulae that renders them unacceptable today is their central reliance on the category of substance. . . . It is as though we were saying that Christ is made out of the same lump of divine substance as the Godhead, and thus shares the divine nature."[6]

If Christians were in fact saying such a thing, then here indeed would be substantial realism with a vengeance! Because, for most theologians, the Aristotelianism of late medieval philosophy is now merely a footnote in histories of doctrine, however, it is obvious to them that the static understanding of *ousia*, on which such an interpretation relied, was a culturally conditioned ontological or metaphysical assumption. With this recognition, it is easier for them to use the patristic theology through which the term first came into use, without imposing on it the substantial overtones of later medieval interpretation. It is also clear that if the patristic framework is to continue in use, such overtones might be most easily avoided through an awareness of problems of translation. (It is notable that in English liturgical translations, for example, the term *ousia* is now frequently rendered—perhaps not without further problems—by "essence" or "being" rather than by "substance.")

Just as that example of substantial realism was once quasi-instinctive, however, and could only be seen for what it was after the downfall of the metaphysical framework that made it possible, so other types of similar metaphysical assumption inevitably remain quasi-instinctive. Just as physicists will, through their "conservative metaphysical predilections," instinctively think of the neutrino in particle terms, so Christian theologians will have aspects of their theoretical models into which a similar conservatism has smuggled a particular ontology.

One aspect of this is related to a comment of Soskice's about the mystic's dubbing event that points to the reality of that which we call God. "We discover," she says, "perhaps to our surprise that the Christian mystic is of all theists the most likely to be a realist, aware of the presence and reality of God, yet aware at the same time of the inability of human speech and thought to contain Him."[7] The way she expands on this negative or apophatic aspect of the mystic's experience of God, however, reflects the way that such apophaticism is often treated in Western systematic theology: merely as a corrective to positive, or cataphatic, theology. By contrast it has been argued—by Vladimir Lossky,[8] in particular—that the mystical tradition generally, and the patristic tradition also (particularly in its Greek dimension) has had a far stronger awareness of the essentially apophatic nature of religious language, and with it a corresponding stress on the dangers of bringing ontological assumptions to theological language.

At least one patristic writer seems to have had an understanding of this apophatic approach, in relation to the language used of the created order, which is reminiscent of that which emerges from a modern criticism of substantial realism. According to Lossky, Saint Basil's approach was one in which "not the divine essence alone but also created essences could not be expressed in concepts. In contemplating any object we analyze its properties; it is this which enables us to form concepts. But this analysis can in no case exhaust the content of the object of perception. There will always remain an 'irrational residue' which escapes analysis and which cannot be expressed in concepts; it is the unknowable depth of things, that which constitutes their true, indefinable essence."[9]

Given the differences between fourth-century Hellenistic philosophy and that of the early twentieth century, this parallel should not, perhaps, be pursued too far in exploring the implications of structural realism for modern theological language use. What can properly be pursued in a general way, however, is the more general apophaticism, or negative theology, of the Eastern Orthodox tradition, which Lossky relates not only to Basil's thought but also to that of the whole Greek patristic tradition. This apophaticism, he says, "is an expression of that fundamental attitude which transforms the whole of theology into a contemplation of the mysteries of revelation. . . . Apophaticism teaches us above all to see a negative meaning in the dogmas of the Church: it forbids us to follow natural ways of thought and to form concepts that would usurp the place of spiritual realities."[10]

This approach (though not without its problems in the late Byzantine version of it espoused by Lossky and his followers)[11] is an extremely attractive one, not least to those who wish to maintain the validity of patristic theology. It may indeed be that an appreciation of the arguments against a substantial realism in the sciences could prove an important contributor to the process of reappropriating this sort of patristic insight. If such a possibility provides comfort for Christian traditionalists who wish to defend the continued use of patristic theology, however, the insights of a structural realism also pose some awkward questions for them, especially in relation to interfaith considerations. Such insights suggest the logical possibility that some of the perceived incompatibilities of the doctrines of different faiths may exist only at the level of those doctrines' substantial interpretation. At the deeper, structural level, such insights suggest, such incompatibilities may seem less definitive or may even disappear altogether.

An example from within the Christian tradition—that of arguments about transubstantiation in the eucharist—sheds light upon the way in which this can happen. For in the context of the Aristotelian metaphysic that we have already noted, the argument about the real presence of Christ in the eucharist was, in the centuries immediately following the Reformation, essentially one about the distinction between "substance" and "accidents." Those who, for whatever reason, believed that the Roman doctrine of change of substance was inadequate, were forced to work out their position within a metaphysical framework which, if it eschewed the Aristotelian system at a formal level, was still essentially that of their opponents, dominated by a particular sort of substantial realism. Both the classical Lutheran position of "consubstantiation" and the Calvinist reaction to it were tied equally to a notion of substance inherited from the scholastic period.[12] By contrast, the kind of eucharistic agreement that has emerged in dialogue between these traditions in recent years has been due precisely to the modern ability to consider the question of the real presence in a different metaphysical context—one in which relational categories are more evident than crude substantial ones.

Such an example—when extrapolated to interfaith dialogue—would seem, at the very least, to constitute a warning that the questions we pose in such dialogue must be carefully examined to avoid the smuggling in of metaphysical assumptions that are secondary to the claims to realism imputed of doctrinal theory. Thus, for example, the emphasis on relational categories fostered by such insights will tend to stress, in such dialogue, the soteriological dimension of doctrine—the relationship of God to humanity and the cosmos—rather than models of the divine abstracted from such considerations. (That this emphasis corresponds to one we have noted in relation to a puzzle-solution methodology is coincidental but, for that very reason, of considerable significance.) Similarly, as we have already observed, questions of how the concept of the "personal" may be used about God may need to be examined extremely carefully to distinguish uses that are at least putatively intrinsic to a referential statement from those that are arbitrary interpretative impositions.

Indeed, interfaith dialogue may well prove the main crucible in which an understanding of structural realism can be forged. Just as it was only encounter with new philosophical systems within the Christian community that allowed the Aristotelian interpretation of "substance" to be seen for what it was, so now both new philosophical insights from outside the world's faiths and encounter with the very different metaphysical systems of other faiths may sharpen our insights into the difference between genuine IP reference and the way that such reference is often expressed in an apparent DC mode through the incorporation of arbitrary metaphysical elements.

If such possibilities form the basis of a research program into the implications of structural realism for an interfaith dialogue based on the type of convergent pluralism discussed previously, however, it is important that one possible misapprehension is avoided. A simplistic reading of the nature of structural realism may give the impression that existing doctrinal languages, with their inevitable substantial interpretations, are potentially redundant in the sense of being replaceable, through convergent dialogue, by a single, purely relational language. Insofar as such a realism emerges from the work of Harré and Hesse on the sciences, however, this is not the case. On the contrary, according to these philosophers of science, the use of substantial models is, in the sciences, a necessary feature of the development and application of scientific theory.

In this sense, to talk, as Hesse does, of substantial models being *interpretations* of structural theories is potentially misleading, unless it is recognized that she does not see such interpretations as secondary in the sense of being impositions onto already-developed theory. Rather, in her view, the substantial "interpretation," as an intrinsic part of the developing model, will have had its part to play in both the evolution and the application of the theory. As Soskice has put it, the model or analogue "forms a living part of the theory, the cutting edge of its capacity and, hence, is indispensable for explanatory and predictive purposes. . . . If the . . . account of . . . Harré and Hesse is correct, then precisely what one cannot do with any living and valuable scientific theory is to make the model separate from and subordinate to it."[13]

Soskice herself, it must be admitted, fails to make an adequate distinction between the status of structural theory and substantial model in terms of realism. Nevertheless, her insight here is an important one in the context in which she uses it—that of attacking the sort of criticism of theological realism associated with people such as Frederick Ferré,[14] based on the assumption that in scientific explanation, models are always subservient to theory and dispensable in favor of pure theory. The inseparability of substantial model and structural theory as components of a research program and as tools for application is such that the theoretical basis of structural realism does not lead to the possibility of a purely relational language cut free entirely from metaphysical assumptions.

What this means in terms of interfaith dialogue is that any convergent pluralism must involve the development of each faith's doctrinal structures in terms of its own existing models. While an appreciation of perspectives from other faiths may suggest important new directions—especially when the arbitrary element of a substantial realism is taken into account—this cannot involve any facile syncretism. Concepts used in any one faith will have a rooting in a substantial model that, even when the arbitrary metaphysical element of the latter is recognized, is likely to make their adoption into another such model far from straightforward.

Having said this, it is perhaps worth noting that this relatively conservative understanding of the implications of structural realism for interfaith dialogue might be considerably modified if the analyses of Harré and Hesse are extended in a way that they themselves might be unwilling to allow. Such a possibility is, however, suggested by others' speculations in similar areas of the philosophy of science.

One approach, which is of particular relevance to theological questions, is through the way in which concepts and ontologies valuable at one stage of scientific exploration are not merely changed subsequently but, like the phlogiston of eighteenth-century chemistry or the *luminiferous aether* of nineteenth-century physics, are actually abandoned. A simplistic defense of causal theories of reference might claim, with one textbook, that "these are not changes of reference . . . the terms in question never did refer."[15] A more nuanced analysis might, however, see in these now outmoded theories a genuine reference to complex relational properties that were, in subsequent theories, referred to in other ways, if only implicitly.

One of the problems of causal theories of reference in their original form has been their stress on entities that can be pointed at rather than ones that may, even in principle, be unobservable. Harré's distinction between DC and IP reference modes goes some way toward remedying this, but there seem still to be cases where reference goes beyond either of these categories. Richard Boyd, in particular, has pointed out that the standard account of causal theories of reference is suited less well to complex scientific reference than to reference involving display of samples of a substance whose real essence is its internal constitution. He points in particular to the way in which, in the sciences, metaphor can be theory constitutive, especially in younger sciences such as cognitive psychology, with its widespread use of computer terminology. The reference in such cases is, he suggests, to "kinds whose real essences consist of complex relational properties, rather than features of internal constitution."[16]

We are now near the frontiers of the development of causal theories of reference, and it would perhaps be just as well not to attempt to anticipate their future in detail. Nevertheless, if we take seriously Boyd's concept of reference to complex relational properties, we can begin to see why the entities of scientific theory cannot merely be given radically different metaphysical interpretations as that theory develops, but can even disappear from theory altogether, their previous status as "substantial" referents having been recognized as being an unnecessary or misleading metaphysical imposition. Thus, for example, the concept of the *luminiferous aether* as the medium through which electromagnetic waves travel can be seen as having given, to use Boyd's phrase, *epistemic access*[17] to the phenomenon of the propagation of such waves through metaphorical comparison with the media through which other types of wave travel. Though disappearing from scientific theory only with the advent of relativity, this aether was not intrinsic to the pre-relativistic theory of electromagnetic waves, but was, nevertheless, an important way, historically, of conceiving the complex relational properties described by that theory.[18]

Such an example seems to point to the way that central concepts of some (especially younger) sciences may, having provided epistemic access to phenomena through metaphor, actually disappear in the subsequent course of theory development. The question that arises from this, for the theologian, is whether similarly central concepts in theology might, even in a critically realist approach, also be susceptible to abandonment. Might we, in fact, see theology as more akin to "younger" sciences—of which Boyd speaks when he talks about the role of metaphor as theory constitutive—than to those more mature ones in which metaphor has an important but more constrained role?

In the context of interfaith dialogue, for example, what is the Christian to make of what John Hick calls "the metaphor of God incarnate?"[19] While Soskice's analysis of metaphor in theological thought would tend to point rather straightforwardly to a realist interpretation of such a metaphor (coupled with a recognition that it might be a mistake), an extended structural realism, of the kind that might emerge from Boyd's analysis, could lead to a far more nuanced realism in which the metaphor, while providing genuine epistemic access to the reality affirmed through it, might at least in principle disappear in its classic form in the course of theory development. (Certainly, the development I have suggested from the doctrine in its classic form to a wider sacramental panentheism has been made possible only because of the epistemic access provided by the doctrine.)

We have seen, then, that the adoption of a critical realism in theology, based on a similar realism in the sciences, is not without its problems. We have noted, however, that recent insights into the nature of scientific realism, expressible in terms of a preference for a structural rather than a substantial realism, allow the nature of some of these problems to be clarified. It seems clear that an understanding of the arguments for such a preference, as they emerge from the analyses of Harré and Hesse, has important implications for those who wish to explore a putative critical realism in theology based on a comparable realism in the sciences.

In particular, such an understanding points toward the need for a greater recognition of the metaphysical assumptions that are both essential to the development of theological language and yet also essentially arbitrary as far as that language's claims to realism are concerned—in that they are susceptible to radical change as that language develops. The implications for a new appreciation of the apophatic nature of such language are considerable. The implications for interfaith dialogue seem even more significant, especially if the work of Boyd on epistemic access is added to what emerges from the analyses of Harré and Hesse. Indeed, it would seem that an understanding of structural realism in the sciences may be able to provide the basis for a realist understanding of religious language that can genuinely address the needs of a pluralistic age.

11

Psychology, Reference, and the Faiths of the World

Our exploration began with some general considerations about the modern dialogue of science and theology and the concepts of divine action that have arisen within it. We noted, in particular, that questions about revelation as an aspect of divine action had emerged from that analysis, and that aspects of human psychology have not only precisely the general characteristics that a pansacramentalist account of revelatory experience requires, but also seem worthy of exploration in historical terms. We also observed that a recognition of the psychological mechanism of revelatory experience is not incompatible with the belief that such experience may manifest genuine reference to an extra-psychic reality. We have also explored ways that this reference could be recognized, in terms of an understanding of the nature of religious language, and have linked them to aspects of recent thought about the concept of revelation.

All of this has suggested that what we might call a *psychological-referential model of revelatory experience* is one that can best provide a basis for an understanding of the nature of revelation. Such a model, as we have seen, is not unconnected to others, in that Keith Ward has already attempted a pluralist model involving "a blend of human imagination and reflection and Divine . . . co-operative persuasion."[1] Similarly, Karl Rahner has explored visionary experience influenced by "elements of phantasy, patterns of perception, selective attitudes of expectation due to religious training . . . etc."[2] In many respects, in fact, the general psychological-referential model presented here could have been formulated as a creative combination of the more fruitful elements of each of these analyses, and in this and possibly other[3] ways its validity could have been urged quite independently of the particular arguments that have led to it in my own presentation. Like the related understanding of the Easter experiences that we have explored, it is robust in the sense of not being dependent on the exact details of my own particular chain of reasoning.

The importance of such a psychological-referential model lies chiefly, it would seem, in the light that it can throw on one of the great problems of our pluralistic age: that of developing an adequate theology of the world's faiths. The main barrier to such a development has, hitherto, been the observation that, unless authentic revelation (taking this term in its widest sense)[4] is regarded as entirely non-referential, it is very difficult to see how it could have given rise to more than one of the faiths of the world. If the languages of these faiths are taken as straightforwardly referential, they are simply incompatible with one another. Unless, therefore, we can find a way of speaking with much greater subtlety about the relationship of revelatory experience to reference than we have done up until now, any attempt at a pluralistic theology of the world's faiths will always stumble when the matter of the "truth claims" of different faiths is raised.

It is precisely here, it would seem, that a two-component, psychological-referential model of revelatory experience is potentially extremely fertile. The apparent link between cultural expectations and the content of psychologically rooted revelatory experience, which we have already noted a number of times in this study, suggests an important distinction between different aspects of such experience. On the one hand, the model suggests, there may be aspects of the experience that are genuinely referential to an extra-psychic reality. On the other, it goes on to assert, there will almost inevitably be aspects that simply reflect cultural expectations, which make that particular type of revelatory experience psychologically possible.

Such a perspective suggests, for example, that if the experiences of the "risen" Christ were, as I have suggested, made psychologically possible by cultural expectations about resurrection, then we must be open to the possibility that some details of that experience—such as the concept of a "resurrection body"—may have no referential status. Rather, that concept might be no more than an aspect of the psychological vehicle for the conveyance of the revelatory experience. This is but an example of the way that, in a two-component, psychological-referential theory of revelation, any referential content in revelatory experiences may, to some extent, be "hidden" within the culturally influenced expectations in and through which that experience is psychologically appropriated. This has the corollary that the doctrine that is initially "read off" from the experience will not necessarily be referential. Rather, whatever its salutary instrumentalist effect at an unconscious level, the perceived content of revelatory experience will be at best only a *candidate* for truly referential doctrine.

If we accept this possibility, however, the ramifications are not limited to marginal concepts, of the type that the resurrection body is often held to be. The two-component model suggests, in addition, at least the logical possibility that the referential content of an authentic revelatory experience may be unrelated to *most* of its details, including those that have traditionally been held as central. Thus, in relation to the Easter experiences, it becomes conceivable that their referential content may not only exclude the concept of Christ's resurrection body, but may also exclude any information at all about his person, in the sense of it being about his status as God incarnate or even as a glorified prophet. The genuine referential content of those experiences might, for example, be related to something much more abstract, such as the provisional nature of death.

If this were the case, however, then it is clear that the reference made available to Christians through the Easter appearances might have been made available to others—partially or wholly—through a completely different revelatory vehicle, with no reference to the person of Jesus at all. If the reference in the resurrection appearance experiences were indeed something rather abstract such as the provisional nature of death, then many religions have, at their heart, some revelatory or enlightening experience related to this concept.

This sort of consideration makes clear how apposite a two-component model of revelatory experience is to the development of a theology of the world's faiths. The revelatory or enlightening experiences from which all the main faiths of the world have emerged are in principle susceptible to analysis in terms of the model. Questions about the referential content of such experiences, as they arise for each faith from such a model, clearly impinge directly on the question of the relationship between those faiths.

Indeed, the three main existing approaches to the nature of doctrine, which already inform attitudes toward this issue, may now be examined from the perspective of a wider framework.

The first of these existing approaches is the exclusivist one, in which all religious traditions but one's own are viewed as inherently inferior. Within a psychological-referential framework, however, this approach would only be justifiable if all revelatory experiences except those at the roots of (or conforming to) one's own faith could be assumed to be "merely" psychological—at best effective at an instrumental level. Only the experiences associated with one's own tradition, in this view, should be seen as referential to an extra-psychic reality. Such a view, when analyzed in terms of a general psychological-referential understanding of revelatory experience, is essentially arbitrary unless, in terms of the criteria set out in our discussion of religious language, it could be demonstrated that the doctrine that has arisen within one's own tradition has greater puzzle-solving ability than that which has arisen elsewhere. Such a demonstration has yet, however, to be made.

The second existing approach to interfaith dialogue is the complete opposite of this exclusivist one. It is the relativist one of viewing all faiths as essentially equal in terms of their referential validity. A psychological-revelatory version of such a view would, presumably, either hold that no faith has arisen from genuinely referential revelation, or else—from the point of view of what has been called a theocentric relativism[5]—that all revelatory experiences have acted equally as signposts to the transcendent dimension of existence, but have no further referential content. The specific differentiating content of the faiths that have emerged from primary revelatory experiences would, for both of these relativistic views, be interpreted in purely instrumentalist terms, and not be susceptible to comparison in terms of the question: Which is true (or at least more true)? From the point of view of a psychological-referential model of revelation, however, these relativist approaches, like the exclusivist one, manifest an essential arbitrariness. While the exclusivist view, on purely subjective grounds, limits referential content to only certain revelatory experiences, almost all relativist ones—though a partial exception should perhaps be made of the approach of John Hick[6]—are equally arbitrary in their refusal to consider any claim to specific referential content.

This refusal has been encouraged in recent years by what is sometimes called a "linguistic" approach to religious life and doctrine, such as that advocated by George Lindbeck.[7] This approach, with its emphasis on the way in which doctrine, religious narrative, ritual, and life orientation are mutually interpenetrating, stresses that religious belief is to be understood primarily in relation to the believing community as manifested in all its activities. Such an emphasis undoubtedly has, in the context of a psychological-referential model, important points, not least in relation to its potential clarification of the cultural dimension of that model. The linguistic view's essentially instrumentalist understanding of doctrine, however, is such that the questions about reference in revelatory experience, which we are addressing here, are simply bypassed. What is surely required—and indeed may be legitimate even in terms of its Wittgensteinian background[8]—is an expansion of the linguistic view in terms of the questions about reference that arise from a psychological-referential model.

Such an expansion would certainly be possible; indeed, it seems to be at least implicit in the third approach to interfaith dialogue that we need to consider. This is the "convergent pluralism," which, as we have noted, while holding that religious languages may make real and explorable referential truth claims, at the same time recognizes the complexity of the way these truth claims have arisen from particular culturally conditioned experiences. The existence of competing religious frameworks necessarily means, in this view, that some religious traditions may possess certain truths (or at least approximations to truth) in greater fullness than do others, but equally means that no one faith can make exclusivist claims.

Certainly, only a pluralist approach of this sort can avoid the essential arbitrariness of the exclusivist and relativist approaches. Thus far, however, the pluralist approach has suffered from a lack of focus on the revelatory or enlightening experiences on which the various faiths of the world are based. This is not because it has followed the relativistic linguistic approach's dogmatic stress on existing religious communities, isolated from the experiences from which those communities emerged. Because there has been no framework within which to carry out a broader analysis, however, the viewpoint of convergent pluralism has in practice failed to address adequately the questions of the nature of those foundational experiences and of their consequent role in interfaith dialogue.

This problem finds a ready resolution in the context of the psychological-referential model that we are exploring here, however, and as a result, it can be argued that an essentially new type of pluralism becomes possible. Such a model suggests that referential truths about some aspect of the divine reality—hidden within culturally conditioned vehicles—may have been vouchsafed in revelatory experience at different times and in different cultures. The differences between those experiences, as we have discussed, may be seen as having been largely determined by the differences between the cultures concerned, with their very different expectations about the nature of salvation and of the ways in which it might be attained or given. Thus the differences between the world's faiths are, for this model, a natural corollary of the psychological mode by which those faiths have been engendered.

In the context of a psychological-referential model, a useful way of thinking about this revelatory aspect of interfaith understanding is, I would suggest, by analogy with the now well-known biological concept of the ecological niche. We may similarly, I suggest, use the concept of the *psycho-cultural niche,* which may be defined by both the cultural assumptions and the individual psychological makeup of those able to experience some religious revelation or enlightenment. Such a concept relates very straightforwardly to the psychological-referential model in that, in such a model, a particular psycho-cultural niche provides the necessary psychological environment for some particular revelation to arise, and also limits the type of experience that could arise and flourish, in a way analogous to that in which a particular ecological niche allows only certain new biological species to emerge and spread.

The analogy here is to the way that we would expect only certain types of species to have emerged in, say, the Polar Regions. Just as polar bears would not have been expected to emerge as a species other than in a polar region, so each of the world's main faiths has been able to emerge only in certain cultures, and within those cultures only in certain individuals. Thus, for example, the revelation manifested in the person of Jesus Christ has often been seen as one that could only have occurred in the Judaistic culture of the first century of the Common Era, with its eschatological and messianic expectations. The concept of the psycho-cultural niche has the advantage, as we have seen, of setting this cultural dimension within a wider psychological understanding of revelation, providing a ready way of visualizing why that particular revelation crystallized not only at a particular point in time and space, but also only with certain individuals in and through a particular sort of experience.

Moreover, because the possibility of religious conversion—the acceptance of a particular revelatory "story"—is clearly linked to those psychological and cultural factors that made possible that story's initial emergence,[9] this model has further explanatory features. Thus, in much the same way that it explains how the Christian revelation could only have arisen within Judaism at a certain stage of its development, it also makes understandable the fact that that revelation had its most profound secondary impact in the Hellenistic and not, for example, in the Far Eastern, world. There is a direct analogy with the reasons that a species would be expected to flourish after its emergence only in a certain type of environment.

Thus, the development of Hellenistic Christianity may be seen, in "niche" terms, as equivalent to the successful adaptation of certain species (sometimes with important modifications) to environments other than those in which they emerged. The failure of Christian evangelism in the Far East can similarly be understood in niche terms, as a failure in adaptation, analogous, for example, to the failure of polar bears to flourish in equatorial Africa. That a biological species is no longer to be found in its original geographical location—because of ecological changes in that location—also has its parallel here. Thus, the dying out of the original Judaistic Christianity may be understood in terms of the way in which the psycho-cultural niche provided by early first-century Judaism was so radically changed, both by the emergence of Christianity and then by the fall of Jerusalem in the year 70 C.E., that Judaistic Christianity could no longer flourish and, in fact, gradually died out.

This use of a biological analogy is, it should be noted, very different from the superficially similar use of such an analogy in Richard Dawkins's discussion of the "meme." Examples of these, says Dawkins, "are tunes, ideas, catch-phrases, clothes fashions, ways of making pots or building arches. Just as genes propagate themselves in the gene pool by leaping from body to body via sperms or eggs, so memes propagate themselves in the meme pool by leaping from brain to brain via a process which, in the broadest sense, can be called imitation."[10] The crucial difference between this meme concept and that of the psycho-cultural niche, however, is that the latter is based on a nonreductionist understanding, while the former is explicitly reductionist. Thus religious belief, in meme terms, is held to be simply a manifestation of the "god meme," whose "survival value . . . in the meme pool results from its great psychological appeal."[11] The concept of the psycho-cultural niche, by contrast, is based on the argument that a revelation—which emerges through psychological mechanisms within such a niche—may have a referential content that is no more reducible to psychology than the life that emerges in a particular ecological niche is reducible to chemistry.

The core of the idea of the psycho-cultural niche is, then, that just as life is potentially multiform, and will arise and develop new forms 'spontaneously' through natural (chemical and biological) processes in accordance with the possibilities inherent in a given ecological environment, so revelation—psychological in mechanism, but also in part genuinely referential—is also potentially multiform. It too will arise and develop new forms 'spontaneously,' through natural (psychological) processes, in accordance with the possibilities inherent in a given cultural and psychological environment. Whether we are considering life or revelation, however, neither spontaneity nor naturalness precludes a theological explanation in terms of divine action through the sacramental potential of the cosmos. Rather, as we have seen from the pansacramental naturalism now arising from the science and religion debate, both life and revelation may be held to represent new irreducible emergents intrinsic to that sacramental potential. As such they remain, in the deepest sense, gifts of God.

What we have also now seen, however, is that revelation may be a far more complex gift than has been generally appreciated. In particular, the question of which aspects of any revelatory experience are genuinely referential, and which are simply part of the psychological vehicle by which they have been appropriated, is not one that can be answered easily. Indeed, I have argued, only in the context of both interfaith dialogue and of a deeper understanding of the mode of reference of religious language, tied to an understanding of the puzzle-solving success of that language, will a coherent answer be possible. The pursuit of such an answer is, however, surely now the most urgent task of philosophical theology. If the conclusions to which I have come are valid, it would seem that they provide a foundation for a new and extremely fruitful understanding of the nature of religious experience and language.

Afterword

Ramon Lull (1232–1316 c.e.) should perhaps be the patron saint of all who seek to enter the kind of interfaith dialogue that, at several points in this study, has been indicated as central to the development of Christian theology. In the context of the period in which he lived, his attempt to initiate such dialogue was simultaneously both audacious in its conception and rigorous in its execution.

Lull was, however, far more than a philosophical theologian. He is now remembered less for his contributions in that area, in fact, than for his mystical writings. In at least some versions of his *Book of the Lover and the Beloved*—a classic of mysticism expounded in a literary form borrowed from Islamic Sufism—is the following passage, which makes clear the wider context in which his intellectual striving took place:

> The Lover entered a beautiful meadow and there he saw many children who were following butterflies and trampling down the flowers. The more the children worked to catch the butterflies, the higher did they fly. And the Lover as he watched them said, "Such are those who with subtle reasoning try to comprehend my Beloved, who opens the doors to the simple and closes them to the subtle. And Faith reveals the secrets of my Beloved through the casement of love."[1]

Given the emphasis on revelation in the present study and on the total (and not just intellectual) human response to it, this passage will, I think, serve better than anything that I could write as an indication of the context in which I hope that my own argument will be considered.

That argument has been, essentially, that an important tendency within the current science and religion debate—that which stresses the action of God in and through the scientifically explorable, natural processes of the cosmos—leads naturally to a psychological understanding of revelation. Such an understanding represents, I have argued, neither a type of natural theology nor a form of deism. Rather, I have suggested, it constitutes a naturalism that reflects a type of sacramental panentheism or pansacramentalism, intrinsic to the patristic and Eastern Orthodox traditions, and is to be found in a developed form in certain authors, such as Arthur Peacocke, who have written on the relationship of science and religion.

Such a psychological model is, I have argued, neither susceptible to a straightforward reductionism nor—certainly in the case of the foundational experience at the heart of the Christian faith—inconsistent with what can be said about the empirical character of that experience. However, I have stressed, an affirmation of revelatory experience as more than simply psychological does require both an acknowledgement of some degree of referential content in those experiences and the development of criteria by which that content can be recognized, at least in principle. Such considerations, I have noted, necessarily imply that interfaith considerations are to be taken into account, not least because such a psychological model involves the recognition of a culturally influenced, essentially instrumentalist component to the doctrine "read off" from revelatory experience. Such a psychological-referential model of revelatory experience might best, I have suggested, be understood in terms analogous to those used for the emergence and development of biological species, so that we might talk of a psycho-cultural niche just as in biology we talk about an ecological one.

The criteria for recognition of the genuinely referential component of revelatory experience could, I have suggested, be best developed in terms of a post-foundationalist "puzzle-solution" methodology, analogous to that found in the sciences according to the post-Kuhnian consensus. Such a methodology, I have noted, has some surprisingly conservative aspects, which are, despite this character, essential even to radical doctrinal change. This methodology would, I have suggested, lead to a focus on certain aspects of patristic and Eastern Orthodox theology, on the one hand, and elements of the science and religion debate, on the other—particularly those that tackle scientific perspectives that seem to offer a real challenge to religious belief.

While such a methodology does not in itself depend on any particular ontological assumptions, I have noted, it requires development, in the context of a psychological-referential model of revelation, in terms of some sort of theological realism. However, I have argued, "critical realism," which is often discussed in relation to the relationship between scientific and theological language usage, requires a fuller understanding than has been evident thus far. Such an understanding, I have suggested, is available through the "structural realism" advocated in the philosophy of science by Mary Hesse, supplemented by aspects of the "referential realism" of Rom Harré. Such a realism in theology, I have noted, has important implications both for interfaith dialogue and for a new appreciation of the essential apophaticism of theological language.

What, then, do such insights imply for the future of theology? It is difficult, in practice, to think of any branch of the subject that would not be radically affected by an acceptance of this thesis. Certainly as far as the dialogue of science and theology is concerned, it suggests the need for a radical reappraisal of the work of the last generation or two. Such a new beginning would not, however, in any way imply that the efforts of previous generations have been wasted. On the contrary. If, starting with inadequate assumptions about both rationality and revelation, those generations have cautiously moved toward a conclusion in which their initial assumptions have proved to be only questionable approximations, that conclusion has enabled a new set of initial assumptions to be formulated. Such a conclusion, about the need for both a richer notion of rationality and for an integration of revelation into a picture of God's action through natural processes, allows the wheel to come full circle, so that the old questions can be asked in a new way.

A new iterative cycle (as a mathematician would call it) must begin in the science and religion debate, with new and better approximations derived from the previous cycle. Precisely how this will be worked out remains to be seen. As far as the articulation of this new understanding of rationality and revelation is concerned, the present study marks only a tentative beginning. At the very least, we might guess, there will need to be a new emphasis on interdisciplinary dialogue with subjects such as psychology, sociology, and anthropology, which deal with those properties that have arisen, in the human being, as irreducible emergent properties of the universe. This new perspective suggests that it is precisely in and through these emergent properties, with their sacramental potential, that God chooses to reveal himself.

There is, of course, an alternative course open to us. It is that of dismissing this whole perspective and of continuing to defend the faith that we have inherited, attempting to refute those apparently heretical possibilities that have emerged in our defense so far. That road is one on which we continue to see the task, as John Polkinghorne apparently still does, as one of exploring "to what extent we can use the search for motivated understanding . . . as a route to being able to make the substance of Christian orthodoxy our own."[2]

Certainly, in comparison with the direction indicated by the conclusions to which I have come, Polkinghorne's road is a more comfortable one—at any rate, for those of us for whom the Christian orthodoxy he defends has been precious. The alternative to that apologetic road is a rock-strewn one, with all the inevitable dangers of a process that is, as Arthur Peacocke has put it, "intended not so much as 'apologetic' but, putatively, as creative theology in response to the comprehensive, indeed dazzling, perspective on the being and becoming of the world and of humanity that the sciences have now unveiled to our generation."[3]

As Peacocke has written elsewhere, that harder road is not one that is likely to lead to a bland restatement of a traditional doctrine. It is, rather, one on which we have "a chance to respond to questions which are actually being asked in the context of our present scientific culture. In responding . . . theology will find that there is scarcely any one of the 'heads' of Christian doctrine, as they used to be called, that is not affected by the new perspective."[4] He himself clearly hopes that "one day a new coherent theology might emerge prompted by this stimulus and so continue in our own day what, for example, the Cappadocian Fathers and St. Thomas Aquinas did in their times in relation to contemporary philosophy and science."[5] It is possible, however—as all that I have said about interfaith considerations indicates—that a new coherent theology of this sort will involve a degree of discontinuity with the Christian past, about which he himself might feel uneasy, and which those former saints of the church would certainly have found unacceptable.

Given this possibility, it is perhaps not entirely clear which of these roads is the more likely to come eventually to a dead end. My own judgment, that the more radical road is the one that will prove the more fruitful, will have been obvious from all that I have written. The different judgment of others will, however, be equally important for the theological enterprise. For, as we have noted, crises in theology have their parallels with those in science, in which conservatives and radicals exist side by side until either the old received framework is seen to have solved the problems that have arisen within it, or else a revolutionary leap of understanding arises from the radical side. My own judgment, that the potential for such a leap now exists, is one that will require the most rigorous possible criticism from the conservative side before it either can or should be generally accepted.

Notes

Preface

1. These are, in the order in which they appeared: "An Authentic Theological Revolution? Scientific Perspectives on the Development of Doctrine," *Journal of Religion* 74 (1994): 524ff.; "A New Deism? Science, Religion and Revelation," *Modern Believing* 36:2 (1995): 38ff.; "Structure Not Substance: Theological Realism for a Pluralistic Age," *International Journal for Philosophy of Religion* 37 (1995): 167ff.; "Resurrection, Religion and 'Mere' Psychology," *International Journal for Philosophy of Religion* 39 (1996): 159ff.; "Psychology, Revelation, and Interfaith Dialogue," *International Journal for Philosophy of Religion* 40 (1996): 147ff.; "The Resurrection as Religious Experience," *Modern Believing* 39:2 (1998): 16ff.; "Natural Religion Revisited: New Perspectives on Revelation," in N. H. Gregersen, U. Gorman, and C. Wasserman, eds., "The Interplay of Scientific and Theological Worldviews" *Studies in Science and Theology* 6 (Geneva, Labor et Fides, 1998).

An earlier paper that introduced this argument was: "Hysteria and Myth: The Psychology of the Resurrection Appearances," *Modern Churchman* 31:2 (1989): 38ff.

Chapter 1

1. K. Ward, *A Vision to Pursue: Beyond the Crisis in Christianity* (London: SCM, 1991), ix.

2. R. Dawkins, *The Blind Watchmaker* (London: Longman, 1986), 38.

3. N. Lash, "Observation, Revelation, and the Posterity of Noah," in R. J. Russell, W. R. Stoeger, and G. V. Coyne, eds., *Physics, Philosophy and Theology: A Common Quest for Understanding* (Vatican City State: Vatican Observatory, 1988), 205, has criticized the term dialogue as suggesting "a

reciprocity or mutuality or influence which the facts belie." The term seems appropriate, however, partly because of the necessary "iterative" procedure that I note below, and partly because of factors associated with the hierarchy of disciplines that I list in chap. 3. In particular, in terms of Lash's question about why there is no observable mutual reciprocity between science and theology, see chap. 8 n. 1.

4. In C. Knight, "A New Deism?—Science, Religion and Revelation," *Modern Believing* 36:4 (1995): 38ff. I was, as far as I know, the first to use this term. Polkinghorne has since objected to the term *apologist* because it seems to imply an attempt "to defend the status quo for its own sake. The question of *truth* is paramount . . ." (*South African Science and Religion Forum Newsletter* 4 [March 1996]: 4). The term as I use it has, however, no such connotation, but simply points to the way in which a perfectly respectable apologetic motivation has an effect on the type of question that seems paramount. This in no sense precludes a genuine search for truth.

5. J. Polkinghorne, *Science and Creation: The Search for Understanding* (London: SPCK, 1988), 15.

6. Lash, "Observation, Revelation," 209.

7. Polkinghorne, *Science and Creation*, 15.

8. For a good account of the interaction of science and theology of this period, see J. H. Brooke, *Science and Religion: Some Historical Perspectives* (Cambridge: Cambridge University Press, 1991), chaps. 5–8.

9. A modern example of a design argument is that associated with the apparent "fine tuning" of the universe to produce conscious beings. See, for example, J. D. Barrow and F. J. Tipler, *The Anthropic Cosmological Principle* (Oxford: Clarendon, 1986).

10. T. F. Torrance, *Reality and Scientific Theology* (Edinburgh: Scottish Academic Press, 1985), 38.

11. J. Barr, *Biblical Faith and Natural Theology* (Oxford: Clarendon, 1993), gives an accessible account both of Barth's approach and of objections to it from the perspective of biblical scholarship.

12. T. F. Torrance, *Space, Time and Incarnation* (Oxford: Oxford University Press, 1969).

13. Torrance, *Reality*, 40.

14. Ibid.

15. These eras witnessed the development of two quite different types of natural theology, the distinction between which is not always fully appreciated in theological comment on the concept of natural theology. The earlier scholastic natural theology was based not on the character of the observed cosmos on which the scientific natural theology of the later

period was based, but on general philosophical arguments. For a good brief account of two of these, and of later critiques of them, see B. Davies, *An Introduction to the Philosophy of Religion*, 2nd ed. (Oxford: Oxford University Press, 1993), chaps. 4 and 5.

16. Torrance, *Reality*, 38.

17. This neglect of epistemological problems seemed justifiable, perhaps because of the attitude toward the realism of theological language that both Peacocke and Polkinghorne adopted. As we shall see in chap. 9, however, the "scientific critical realism" on which both of them based this attitude is not as straightforward as either one believes.

18. J. Polkinghorne, *Scientists as Theologians: A Comparison of the Writings of Ian Barbour, Arthur Peacocke and John Polkinghorne* (London: SPCK, 1996), 6.

19. See for example, I. Barbour, *Religion in an Age of Science: The Gifford Lectures 1989–1991*, vol. 1 (London: SCM, 1990), 3ff.

20. Polkinghorne, *Scientists*, 6–7.

21. Ibid., 7. See also 81ff.

22. A. R. Peacocke, *God and the New Biology* (London: J. M. Dent & Sons, 1986), 30.

Chapter 2

1. A. R. Peacocke, sermon presented in King's College Chapel, Cambridge, 2 March 1997; quoted by permission of the author.

2. Ibid. A revised and expanded version is given in Peacocke's "Biology and a Theory of Evolution," *Zygon* 34:4 (1999), 696.

3. For early examples of this emphasis, see A. R. Peacocke, *Creation and the World of Science: The Bampton Lectures, 1978* (Oxford: Clarendon, 1979), and J. Polkinghorne, *Science and Creation*.

4. The sort of vitalism that required something "extra" to be added to the material world was not, it should be noted, solely the product of religious apologetic. The vitalist theories of Hans Driesch and of Henri Bergson, for example, were essentially of a philosophical nature. For a brief account of vitalist views of evolutionary emergence, see A. R. Peacocke, *God and the New Biology* (London: J. M. Dent & Sons, 1986), 73ff.

5. A. L. Moore, *Science and Faith* (London: Kegan Paul, Trench & Co., 1889), 184. The emphasis on immanence, with its roots in the catholic strand of Anglicanism, is, as we shall see, at the heart of much that has been most fruitful in the dialogue of science and theology. Historically, however, this strand of Anglicanism was not alone in welcoming the Darwinian perspective; in some respects, it paralleled a positive Calvinist response, which

perceived in evolutionary theory the possibility of emphasis on the sovereignty of God. See, for example, J. R. Moore, *The Post-Darwinian Controversies* (Cambridge: Cambridge University Press, 1979).

6. J. Polkinghorne, *Scientists as Theologians: A Comparison of the Writings of Ian Barbour, Arthur Peacocke and John Polkinghorne* (London: SPCK, 1996), 41.

7. For a general discussion of the inherent creativity of the cosmos from a scientific rather than a theological perspective, see P. Davies, *The Cosmic Blueprint* (London: Unwin Hyman, 1987).

8. A. R. Peacocke, *Theology for a Scientific Age: Being and Becoming—Natural, Divine and Human*, enlarged ed. (London: SCM, 1993), 65, 119. See Polkinghorne, *Scientists,* 30–41, for a brief account of the different nuances of approach within this framework to be found in the works of Peacocke, Barbour, and himself.

9. F. Watts, "Science and Theology as Complementary Perspectives," in N. H. Gregersen and J. W. van Huyssteen, ed., *Rethinking Theology and Science: Six Models for the Current Dialogue* (Grand Rapids & Cambridge: Eerdmans, 1998), 157ff.

10. J. Polkinghorne, *One World: The Interaction of Science and Theology* (London: SPCK, 1986), 74ff.

11. Peacocke, *Creation,* 240. For a brief account of how this model relates to a number of contemporary positions, see D. R. Copestake, "Emergent Evolution and the Incarnation of Jesus Christ," *Modern Believing* 36:4 (1995): 27ff.

12. See Polkinghorne, *Scientists.* His comments on Christology, 64ff., are of particular interest.

13. J. Polkinghorne, *Science and Christian Belief: Theological Reflections of a Bottom-Up Thinker* (London: SPCK, 1994), 78–79.

14. Polkinghorne, *Scientists,* 40.

15. A. R. Peacocke, "God's Interaction with the World: The Implications of Deterministic 'Chaos' and of Interconnected and Interdependent Complexity," in R. J. Russell, N. Murphy and A. R. Peacocke, eds., *Chaos and Complexity: Scientific Perspectives on Divine Action* (Vatican City State: Vatican Observatory, 1995), 283.

16. Polkinghorne, *Scientists,* 26ff.

17. B. Davies, *An Introduction to the Philosophy of Religion,* 2nd ed. (Oxford: Oxford University Press, 1993), 141.

18. See, for example, A. M. Farrer, *A Science of God?* (London: Geoffrey Bles, 1968).

19. Thomas Aquinas, *Commentary on Aristotle's Peri Hermeneias,* 1:14, quoted in B. Davies, *Philosophy of Religion,* 153.

20. J. Moltmann, *The Crucified God* (London: SCM, 1974); W. H. Vanstone, *Love's Endeavour, Love's Expense* (London: Darton, Longman & Todd, 1977). The latter—a popular account by a parish priest rather than by a professional theologian—has had a surprisingly strong influence within the small "science and religion" circle of British theologians. See Peacocke, *Theology,* 123ff.; D. Stanesby, *Science, Religion and Reason* (London: Routledge, 1985), 128ff.

21. Peacocke, "God's Interaction," 283.

22. One possibility of describing "providential response" within a single act model of divine action lies in the complex interaction of mind and matter, which in Jungian psychology is described in terms of "synchronicity." While at present such a concept can do no more than point toward the sort of "meaningful coincidence" that many have affirmed as part of their own experience, it does suggest a way such coincidence may be interpreted naturalistically, rather than in terms of supernatural intervention. Extraordinary events that would be described as miraculous in a supernaturalist context might also be understood in similar terms. From a scientific perspective, it is interesting that speculations of this sort are to be found in D. Bohm, *Wholeness and the Implicate Order* (London: Routledge & Kegan Paul, 1980), in which it is suggested, "If matter and consciousness . . . could be understood together, in terms of the . . . notion of order, the way would be open to comprehending their relationship on the basis of a common ground" (197). This comment may be compared to C. G. Jung's postulate— in *Flying Saucers: A Modern Myth of Things Seen in the Sky* (London: Routledge & Kegan Paul, 1959)—of a total reality "grounded on an as yet unknown substrate possessing material and at the same time psychic qualities" (145).

23. J. R. Lucas, "The Temporality of God," in R. J. Russell, N. Murphy, and C. J. Isham, eds., *Quantum Cosmology and the Laws of Nature: Scientific Perspectives on Divine Action* (Vatican City State: Vatican Observatory, 1993), 236.

24. Peacocke, *Theology,* 111.

25. Ibid., 112.

26. Peacocke, "God's Interaction," 238.

27. See, for example, C. J. Isham and J. C. Polkinghorne, "The Debate Over the Block Universe," in Russell et al., *Quantum Cosmology,* 135ff. One thing that is clear from the scientific perspective, irrespective of one's view

of God's timelessness, is that much of the philosophical argument against that timelessness is scientifically illiterate in its failure to recognize that in the perspective of Einstein's physics, time is an aspect of the created order, not something independent of that order.

28. A good overview of this issue, which defends the view of God's timelessness, is given in Davies, *Philosophy of Religion,* 141.

29. The scientific argument against the "response within time" whole-part constraint scheme lies in the way there must always be an extremely long delay between action and result. This comes about because information cannot, from the perspective of relativistic physics, travel at a velocity greater than that of light. If the "whole" involved is the entire cosmos, this means that the delay will normally be of the order of the age of the universe, so that God's "response" to any particular situation seems to require that he has "anticipated" the situation in a way that seems more consonant with the single act account than with that which Peacocke defends. For response within a given time t, only God's effect upon those parts of the universe within distance ct can be effective (where c is the velocity of light), which effectively makes divine action "local" for any reasonable response time.

30. Peacocke, *God and New Biology,* 124.

31. P. Clayton, *God and Contemporary Science* (Edinburgh: Edinburgh University Press, 1997), 82ff., makes a clearer *theological* case for the panentheistic position than does Peacocke himself, and clearly indicates why this position transcends the choice between classical Western theism and pantheism. However, Clayton's own approach does not have the same sacramentalist roots as does Peacocke's.

32. See, for example, Peacocke, *Theology,* 340ff., for comments related to the work of Eastern Orthodox theologians John Zizioulas and Symeon Lash.

33. A Schmemann, *The World as Sacrament* (London: Darton, Longman & Todd, 1966), 19.

34. V. Lossky, *The Mystical Theology of the Eastern Church* (Cambridge: James Clarke, 1957), 101.

35. W. Drees, *Religion, Science and Naturalism* (Cambridge: Cambridge University Press, 1996), 249.

36. Ibid., 251.

37. See D. Barrow and F. J. Tipler, *The Anthropic Cosmological Principle* (Oxford: Clarendon, 1986). J. Polkinghorne, *Reason and Reality* (London: SPCK, 1991), 80, argues, in terms of his attempt at a "revised natural theology," that there is "a meta-question arising from Anthropic Principle con-

siderations to which theism provides a persuasive (but not logically coercive) answer."

38. Lossky's comments about the Western concept of pure nature really only apply to the later scholastics and their successors. In Aquinas, for example, the concept of the supernatural is far more subtle.

39. Peacocke, *Theology*, 202.

40. K. Ward, *Religion and Revelation: A Theology of Revelation in the World's Religions* (Oxford: Clarendon, 1994), 301. This study will be examined in some detail in chap. 6.

Chapter 3

1. For the historical-critical background to this problem, see W. Marxsen, *The Resurrection of Jesus of Nazareth* (London: SCM, 1970) and C. F. Evans, *Resurrection and the New Testament* (London: SCM, 1970).

2. In the earlier part of the century it was common to point to anthropological analyses of such things as the resurrection of Attis—see, for example, J. G. Frazer, *The Golden Bough*, abr. (London: Macmillan, 1957), 461—as indicating the origin of the biblical resurrection appearance accounts. Since that time, however, anthropology has become much more sophisticated and cautious in drawing parallels between different cultures and mythological systems.

3. For a popular account of this approach, see B. L. Mack, *The Lost Gospel* (Longmead: Element Books, 1993).

4. N. Perrin, *The Resurrection Narratives—A New Approach* (London: SCM, 1977).

5. C. Knight, "Hysteria and Myth: The Psychology of the Resurrection Appearances," *Modern Churchman* 31:2 (1989): 38ff.

6. See, for example, S. T. Davis, D. Kendall, and G. O'Collins, eds., *The Resurrection: An Interdisciplinary Symposium on the Resurrection of Jesus* (Oxford: Oxford University Press, 1997), for a flavor of the current debate. As John Wilkins puts it in his contribution, "A Summit Observed," "The divisions . . . were not between those who thought the resurrection 'happened' and those who did not. Rather, they tended to be between the philosophers of religion and the biblical exegetes" (3).

7. See, for example, J. J. Kelly, *Baron Friedrich von Hügel's Philosophy of Religion* (Leuven: Leuven University Press, 1983).

8. See N. Sagovsky, *Between Two Worlds: George Tyrrell's Relationship to the Thought of Matthew Arnold* (Cambridge: Cambridge University Press, 1983).

9. See N. Lash, *Easter in Ordinary* (London: SCM, 1988), 150, for a comment on von Hügel's reliance on positivistic conceptions. In relation both

to religious experience in general and to the nature of religious language (to be taken up in the present essay in chaps. 6 to 10), Lash's comments in this study are of considerable interest.

10. Tyrrell's work has been interestingly analyzed in terms of the Lakatosian conception of a research program (of the type to be discussed here in chap. 5) in N. Murphy, *Theology in an Age of Scientific Reasoning* (Ithaca: Cornell University Press, 1990), 96ff.

11. L. Bouyer, *Rite and Man: The Sense of the Sacral and Christian Liturgy* (London: Burns & Oates, 1963), 1–2.

12. This development has, in fact, acted as an important bridge to the approach we have noted in Peacocke. The legitimacy of this bridge will be argued in chap. 8.

13. Bouyer, *Rite and Man*, 3.

14. Ibid.

15. Ibid.

16. Ibid., 2.

17. K. Rahner, "Visions and Prophecies," in *Studies in Modern Theology* (Heidelberg: Herder & London/Burns & Oates, 1965), 95–96; emphasis added.

18. Ibid., 97.

19. Ibid.

20. Ibid., 114.

21. Ibid., 118–19.

22. See, for example, C. G. Jung, *Flying Saucers: A Modern Myth of Things Seen in the Sky* (London: Routledge & Kegan Paul, 1959), for a psychological account of multiple visionary experience; compare the analysis of religious visions in these terms in Knight, "Hysteria".

23. Rahner, "Visions," 122.

24. C. F. Schiavone, *Rationality and Revelation in Rahner* (New York: Peter Lang, 1994), 229.

25. L. O'Donovan, "Karl Rahner: Foundations of Christian Faith," in *Religious Studies Review* 5 (1979): 198.

26. Schiavone, *Rationality*, 238.

27. Rahner, "Visions," 138–39.

28. H. Urs von Balthasar, *The Glory of the Lord: A Theological Aesthetics,* vol. 1, *Seeing the Form,* trans. E. Laiva-Merikakis (Edinburgh: T & T Clark, 1982), 415–16.

29. E. Schillebeeckx, *Interim Report on the Books Jesus and Christ* (London: SCM, 1980), 80–81.

30. Ibid.

Chapter 4

1. C. G. Jung, *Collected Works*, vol. 11 (London: Routledge & Kegan Paul, 1953–1979), par. 9, 10.

2. Ibid.

3. Ibid., vol. 12, par. 757.

4. Peacocke, *God and New Biology*, 6.

5. P. Davies, *The Cosmic Blueprint* (London: Unwin Hyman, 1987), 143.

6. R. Dawkins, *The Selfish Gene* (Oxford: Oxford University Press, 1967), 207.

7. A. R. Peacocke, *God and the New Biology* (London: J. M. Dent & Sons, 1986), 30.

8. C. S. Lewis, *Surprised by Joy* (London: Geoffrey Bles, 1955), 222.

9. Ibid.

10. Ibid.

11. C. G. Jung, *Flying Saucers: A Modern Myth of Things Seen in the Sky* (London: Routledge & Kegan Paul, 1959).

12. In C. Knight, "Hysteria and Myth: The Psychology of the Resurrection Appearances," *Modern Churchman* 31:2 (1989) 38ff. I have argued that a more compelling but ultimately indecisive version of the argument from history can be constructed. I have not repeated it here, however, as it is not strictly relevant to the argument of this essay.

13. R. Swinburne, *Revelation: From Metaphor to Analogy* (Oxford: Clarendon, 1992), 90.

14. As we noted in chap. 1, such occurrences, in the type of model we are exploring, would correspond, as Polkinghorne has stressed, to changes of "regime" in physical systems, such as that which occurs in certain materials when below a certain temperature they become superconducting. The sort of mind-matter interaction discussed in chap. 2 n. 22 perhaps provides the best starting point for a discussion of this type of phenomenon.

15. See B. Davies, *An Introduction to the Philosophy of Religion*, 2nd ed. (Oxford: Oxford University Press, 1993), 190ff., for a good, brief account of the problems associated with the concept of miracle, including a summary of the classic eighteenth-century critique of David Hume.

Chapter 5

1. D. A. Pailin, "The Confused and Confusing Story of Natural Religion," *Religion* 24 (1994) 208ff., notes no less than eleven fundamentally different uses of the term *natural religion* and rightly comments that "in view of the complex variety of ways in which the term . . . has been understood and of

the fact that some who use it intend thereby more than one of these distinct meanings, it is not surprising that many debates about natural religion have been at cross purposes."

2. Although the term *natural grace* is used in circles influenced by the creation spirituality associated with Matthew Fox, it is used here in the more limited sense that emerges from the sort of sacramental panentheism that has been outlined. While an analysis of the relationship between the two approaches would certainly find parallels between the two, there seem also to be aspects of Fox's approach that are open to criticism, and a coincidence in terminology should not be interpreted as a coincidence in understanding.

3. *Oxford English Dictionary.*

4. J. Barr, "Revelation in History," in *The Interpreter's Dictionary of the Bible*, supp. vol. (Nashville: Abingdon, 1976), 746.

5. See, for example, J. Barr, "Biblical Theology," in *The Interpreter's Dictionary of the Bible*, supp. vol. (Nashville: Abingdon, 1976), 104ff.

6. D. Kelsey, *The Uses of Scripture in Recent Theology* (London: SCM, 1975), 32.

7. R. Swinburne, *Revelation: From Metaphor to Analogy* (Oxford: Clarendon, 1992), 4.

8. See the comments on Swinburne's concept of "propositional revelation" in chap. 6.

9. Swinburne, *Revelation*, 4.

10. N. Sagovsky, *Between Two Worlds: George Tyrrell's Relationship to the Thought of Matthew Arnold* (Cambridge: Cambridge University Press, 1983), 128–29.

11. P. Sherry, *Religion, Truth and Language-Games* (London: Macmillan, 1977), provides a good introduction to the application of Wittgenstein's insights to questions of religious language.

12. D. Stanesby, *Science, Religion and Reason* (London: Routledge, 1985), 173ff., gives a good account of the inherent contradictions of the instrumentalist approach of D. Z. Phillips.

13. A. J. Ayer, *Language, Truth and Logic*, rev. ed. (London: Gollancz, 1946), 114ff.

14. K. R. Popper, *The Logic of Scientific Discovery* (London: Hutchison, 1959); originally published as *Logik der Forschung* (Vienna: J. Springer, 1934).

15. Stanesby, *Science*, gives perhaps the best of the Popperian accounts of theological rationality.

16. A. Flew and A. McIntyre, eds., *New Essays in Philosophical Theol-*

ogy (London: SCM, 1955), contains a number of essays that express this view.

17. I. Lakatos, "Falsification and the Methodology of Scientific Research Programmes," in I. Lakatos and A. Musgrave, eds., *Criticism and the Growth of Knowledge* (Cambridge: Cambridge University Press, 1970), 91ff.

18. N. Murphy, *Theology in an Age of Scientific Reasoning* (Ithaca: Cornell University Press, 1990). This analysis is in many respects an impressive one, but it lacks full persuasiveness partly because it bypasses questions about reference, as we shall see in chap. 9, and partly because it underestimates some of the shortcomings of Lakatos's approach. For an account of these shortcomings, see I. Hacking, *Representing and Intervening* (Cambridge: Cambridge University Press, 1983), 112ff.

19. T. S. Kuhn, *The Structure of Scientific Revolutions* (Chicago: University of Chicago Press, 1962).

20. P. Feyerabend, *Against Method*, rev. ed. (London: Verso, 1988), 1. It should be noted, however, that much of the dismissive comment on Feyerabend seems to ignore aspects of his work that are more conservative, such as his belief (see chap. 6 n. 10) in the comparability of incommensurable theories.

21. See, for example, A. E. McGrath, *The Foundations of Dialogue in Science and Religion* (Oxford: Blackwell, 1998).

22. See, for example, W. H. Newton-Smith, *The Rationality of Science* (London: Routledge & Kegan Paul, 1981); R. Trigg, *Rationality and Science: Can Science Explain Everything?* (Oxford: Blackwell, 1993). Much of what has been most fruitful in recent analysis was anticipated in M. Polanyi, *Personal Knowledge* (London: Routledge and Kegan Paul, 1958).

23. McGrath, *Foundations*, 11.

24. Ibid. The quotation is from S. Connor, *Postmodernist Culture: An Introduction to Theories of the Contemporary* (Oxford: Blackwell, 1989), 35.

25. J. W van Huyssteen, "Postfoundationalism in Theology and Science," in N. H. Gregersen and J. W. van Huyssteen, eds., *Rethinking Theology and Science: Six Models for the Current Dialogue* (Grand Rapids: Eerdmans, 1998), 36. (All future references to van Huyssteen refer to this short essay, which constitutes the best brief introduction to his views. Those who wish to explore these views in more detail are advised to read his *Essays in Postfoundationalist Theology* [1997] from the same publisher.)

26. Ibid.

27. Ibid., 37.

28. Four recent approaches that give a good flavor of both the strengths and weaknesses of current defenses of the rationality of theology are: M.

Banner, *The Justification of Science and the Rationality of Religious Belief* (Oxford: Clarendon, 1990); P. Clayton, *Explanation from Physics to Theology: An Essay in Rationality and Religion* (New Haven: Yale University Press, 1989); Murphy, *Theology*; Stanesby, *Science*.

29. I. Barbour, *Religion in an Age of Science: The Gifford Lectures 1989–1991*, vol. 1 (London: SCM, 1990), 34.

30. Ibid.

31. Ibid., 39.

32. Ibid.

Chapter 6

1. A. R. Peacocke, *God and the New Biology* (London: J. M. Dent & Sons, 1986), 30.

2. J. W van Huyssteen, "Postfoundationalism in Theology and Science," in N. H. Gregersen and J. W. van Huyssteen, eds., *Rethinking Theology and Science: Six Models for the Current Dialogue* (Grand Rapids: Eerdmans, 1998), 40.

3. I. Barbour, *Religion in an Age of Science: The Gifford Lectures 1989–1991*, vol. 1 (London: SCM, 1990), 39.

4. W. Stoeger, "Contemporary Cosmology and Its Implications for the Science-Religion Dialogue," in R. J. Russell, W. R. Stoeger, and G. Koyne, eds., *Physics, Philosophy and Theology: A Common Quest for Understanding* (Rome: Vatican Observatory, 1988), 232–33.

5. van Huyssteen, "Postfoundationalism," 44.

6. P. Clayton, *Explanation from Physics to Theology: An Essay in Rationality and Religion* (New Haven: Yale University Press, 1989), 100.

7. Ibid., 115.

8. Much of Dawkins's popularizing of neo-Darwinian theory is, it must be said, excellent. When he occasionally alludes to religious belief in his formal work, however—as in his analysis of it in terms of his concept of the meme (see chap. 11)—he often manifests an uncharacteristically simplistic approach. In some of his less formal pronouncements (in letters to the press and so on), this occasionally borders on fatuity.

9. S. Carter, "Every star shall sing a carol," to be found, for example, as hymn 354 in *Hymns Ancient and Modern New Standard* (London: Hymns Ancient & Modern Ltd., 1983). One stanza questions:

Who can tell what other cradle
high above the milky way

still may rock the King of Heaven
on another Christmas Day?

10. P. K. Feyerabend, "Reply to Criticism—Comments on Smart, Sellars and Putnam," in his *Realism, Rationalism and Scientific Method: Philosophical Papers,* vol. 1 (Cambridge: Cambridge University Press, 1981), 104ff. Despite seeing all terms as theoretical, he argues, "it is possible to use incommensurable theories for the purpose of mutual criticism" (117), in part, at least, because "both theories may be able to reproduce the 'local grammar' of sentences that are directly connected with observational procedures" (116).

11. A. Nichols, *Yves Congar* (Wilton, Conn.: Morehouse-Barlow, 1989), provides a useful brief introduction to Congar's work.

12. Quoted by W. Henn, "The Hierarchy of Truths According to Yves Congar, O.P.," *Analecta Gregoriana* 246 (1987): 115. Henn's is probably the best introduction to those aspects of Congar's thought that are relevant to this essay.

13. Ibid., 114ff.

14. Ibid., 109–10.

15. Ibid., 115.

16. See C. G. Jung, *Flying Saucers: A Modern Myth of Things Seen in the Sky* (London: Routledge & Kegan Paul, 1959), for an account of how, in Jungian psychology, cultural specificity may be seen as affecting the manifestations of what Jungian psychology sees as ahistorical archetypes of the collective unconscious.

17. See Nichols, *Yves Congar,* 18ff., for a brief account of the psychological structure of the act of faith according to Congar.

18. K. Rahner, "Visions and Prophecies," in *Studies in Modern Theology* (Heidelberg: Herder & London/Burns & Oates, 1965), 97.

19. K. Ward, *Religion and Revelation: A Theology of Revelation in the World's Religions* (Oxford: Clarendon, 1994), 24.

20. Ibid., 91 n. 73.

21. Ibid., 231–32.

22. D. S. Russell, *The Jews from Alexander to Herod* (Oxford: Clarendon, 1967), 148.

23. See, for example, J. M. Robinson, "Ascension," in *The Interpreter's*

Dictionary of the Bible (Nashville: Abingdon, 1962).

24. Ibid.

Chapter 7

1. K. Ward, *A Vision to Pursue: Beyond the Crisis in Christianity* (London: SCM, 1991), vii.

2. Ibid., 175. It should be noted, perhaps, that in some of Ward's later work—particularly in *Religion and Revelation*—he has recognized that this statement is oversimplified, failing to take into full account the cultural rootedness of religious traditions.

3. Ibid., x.

4. Ibid.

5. See, for example, N. Murphy, *Theology in an Age of Scientific Reasoning* (Ithaca: Cornell University Press, 1990). See also chap. 5 n. 18.

6. See, for example, J. Leplin, ed., *Scientific Realism* (Berkeley: University of California Press, 1984).

7. L. Laudan, *Progress and Its Problems* (Berkeley: University of California Press, 1977). It should perhaps be emphasized at this point that I am not taking up a specifically Kuhnian or Laudanian approach, both of which are open to a number of objections—see, for example, in relation to Laudan, P. K. Feyerabend, "More Clothes from the Emperor's Bargain Basement," in his *Problems of Empiricism: Philosophical Papers*, vol. 2 (Cambridge: Cambridge University Press, 1981), 231ff. In particular, as will become clear, I do not accept Laudan's or Kuhn's complete divorce of progress from truth. In what follows I shall, all the same, refer to Kuhn extensively, because his real insights into the nature of science as a puzzle-solving activity have often been overlooked or caricatured, not so much by philosophers of science themselves as by theologians who have used their work.

8. See, for example, W. H. Newton-Smith, *The Rationality of Science* (London: Routledge & Kegan Paul, 1981).

9. See, for example, B. Davies, *An Introduction to the Philosophy of Religion*, 2nd ed. (Oxford: Oxford University Press, 1993), 32ff.

10. J. W van Huyssteen, "Postfoundationalism in Theology and Science," in N. H. Gregersen and J. W. van Huyssteen, eds., *Rethinking Theology and Science: Six Models for the Current Dialogue* (Grand Rapids: Eerdmans, 1998), 46.

11. Ibid., 44.

12. Ibid., 42.

13. See, for example, *The Apocryphal New Testament* and E. Pagels, *The Gnostic Gospels* (New York: Random House, 1979).

14. D. S. Wallace-Hadrill, *The Greek Patristic View of Nature* (Manchester: Manchester University Press, 1968), chap. 5.

15. See especially V. Lossky, *The Mystical Theology of the Eastern Church* (Cambridge: James Clarke, 1957), 9–10; also J. Pelikan, *The Emergence of the Catholic Tradition (100–600)* (Chicago: University of Chicago Press, 1971), 233–34, 265–66, 344–45. For the soteriological background to Arianism, see R. C. Gregg and D. E. Groh, *Early Arianism—A View of Salvation* (London: SCM, 1981).

16. Ward, *A Vision*, 54. It should be noted that in his more recent work—*Religion*—Ward takes a rather more sympathetic attitude toward the doctrine of the incarnation.

17. See, for example, C. Yannaras, *The Freedom of Morality* (Crestwood: St. Vladimir's Seminary Press, 1984).

18. See, for example, J. Zizioulas, *Being as Communion* (London: Darton, Longman & Todd, 1985).

19. V. Lossky, *In the Image and Likeness of God* (London: Mowbray, 1975), 185.

20. See, for example, J. Moltmann, *The Trinity and the Kingdom of God* (London: SCM, 1981).

21. This statement is expanded in what follows, some of which takes its bearings from T. S. Kuhn, *The Structure of Scientific Revolutions* (Chicago: University of Chicago Press, 1962), 98ff. Here Kuhn notes the influence of early logical positivism on members of an earlier generation of philosophers of science who were reluctant to allow the validity of applying a scientific theory beyond the range of data from which it arose. The implicit positivism of certain strands of modern theology is perhaps not uninfluential in the reluctance of many theologians to apply doctrine in a similar way.

22. Kuhn, *Scientific Revolutions*, 151–52.

Chapter 8

1. The autonomy of the sciences in their own sphere can be preserved, in this scenario, through an understanding of theology as taking the highest position in the hierarchy of disciplines, in the way already outlined (chap. 3) in terms of the work of A. R. Peacocke, described briefly in his *God and the New Biology* (London: J. M. Dent & Sons, 1986), chaps. 1 and 2, and expanded in his *Theology for a Scientific Age: Being and Becoming—Natural, Divine and Human*, enlarged ed. (London: SCM, 1993). In the type of hierarchy he analyzes, any discipline is effectively autonomous with respect to disciplines in a higher position in the hierarchy, but not with respect to

those lower. Thus, for example, physics will be autonomous with respect to biology, but the reverse will not be true. In this view of the relation of theology to the sciences, theology itself must take into account all the sciences, but the sciences themselves, in their own spheres, operate independently of theology.

2. T. F. Torrance, *Reality and Scientific Theology* (Edinburgh: Scottish Academic Press, 1985), 39.

3. See, for example, T. F. Torrance, *Theology in Reconciliation* (London: Geoffrey Chapman, 1975).

4. J. Polkinghorne, *Science and Creation: The Search for Understanding* (London: SPCK, 1988), 51–52.

5. Ibid., 2.

6. A. R. Peacocke, *Creation and the World of Science: The Bampton Lectures, 1978* (Oxford: Clarendon, 1979), 187.

7. See J. Dourley, *The Illness That We Are: A Jungian Critique of Christianity* (Toronto: Inner City Books, 1984), for a stimulating general challenge to theology from one school of psychological thought.

8. J. Monod, *Chance and Necessity* (London: Collins, 1972).

9. Peacocke, *God and New Biology*, 128.

10. T. S. Kuhn, *The Structure of Scientific Revolutions* (Chicago: University of Chicago Press, 1962), 169.

11. D. R. Copestake, "Emergent Evolution and the Incarnation of Jesus Christ," *Modern Believing* 36:4 (1995): 27ff., links Peacocke's christological understanding to G. H. W. Lampe's pneumatological approach, fruitfully suggesting further ways in which an evolutionary Christology may be linked to wider theological issues.

12. Peacocke, *God and New Biology*, 82.

13. K. Ward, *A Vision to Pursue: Beyond the Crisis in Christianity* (London: SCM, 1991), 176.

14. Barbour, *Religion*, 90.

Chapter 9

1. See especially A. R. Peacocke, *Intimations of Reality* (Notre Dame: University of Notre Dame Press, 1985); J. M. Soskice, *Metaphor and Religious Language* (Oxford: Clarendon, 1985); J. Polkinghorne, *Reason and Reality* (London: SPCK, 1991).

2. A. E. McGrath, *The Foundations of Dialogue in Science and Religion* (Oxford: Blackwell, 1998), 14.

3. Ibid.

4. T. S. Kuhn, *The Structure of Scientific Revolutions* (Chicago: University of Chicago Press, 1962), 206–7 n. 132.

5. See, for example, L. Laudan, "A Refutation of Convergent Realism," in Leplin, *Scientific Realism*, 218ff.

6. "Introduction" to J. Leplin, ed., *Scientific Realism* (Berkeley: University of California Press, 1984), 4.

7. I. Barbour, *Religion in an Age of Science: The Gifford Lectures 1989–1991*, vol. 1 (London: SCM, 1990), 43.

8. Leplin, "Introduction," 1.

9. N. Murphy, *Theology in an Age of Scientific Reasoning* (Ithaca: Cornell University Press, 1990), 198. For her own analysis of the problematic nature of critical realism, see her "From Critical Realism to a Methodological Approach: Response to Robbins, Van Huyssteen and Heffner," *Zygon* 23 (1988): 287ff.

10. Soskice, *Metaphor*.

11. A. R. Peacocke, *Intimations of Reality* (Notre Dame: University of Notre Dame Press, 1985).

12. See, for example, S. P. Schwartz, ed., *Naming, Necessity, and Natural Kinds* (Ithaca: Cornell University Press, 1977).

13. R. Harré, *Varieties of Realism: A Rationale for the Natural Sciences* (Oxford: Basil Blackwell, 1986), 101ff.

14. Ibid., 316, referring to D. Bohm, *Wholeness and the Implicate Order* (London: Routledge & Kegan Paul, 1980).

15. Ibid., 316.

16. M. B. Hesse, "Physics, Philosophy and Myth," in R. J. Russell, W. R. Stoeger, and G. V. Coyne, eds., *Physics, Philosophy and Theology: A Common Quest for Understanding* (Vatican City State: Vatican Observatory, 1988) 188.

17. Ibid., 187.

18. Ibid., 188.

Chapter 10

1. A. R. Peacocke, *Intimations of Reality* (Notre Dame: University of Notre Dame Press, 1985), 42.

2. J. M. Soskice, *Metaphor and Religious Language* (Oxford: Clarendon, 1985), 152 n.

3. The difference between Buddhist and Christian religious experience is not, of course, simply one of interpretation, in that cultural presuppositions—as we noted in chap. 7 and will note again in an interfaith context in chap. 11—have a direct effect on such experience, prior to interpretation of

it. This does not, however, rule out similarities in experience, so that, for example, some Christian experiences are of a "Buddhist" type, in that they are not intrinsically ones of "personal" encounter with God, even though there will be a tendency to interpret their content in terms of such encounter.

4. Soskice, *Metaphor*, 152.

5. Ibid.

6. J. Hick, "Christology at the Crossroads," in F. G. Healey, ed., *Prospect for Theology: Essays in Honour of H. H. Farmer* (Biswell Place, U. K.: Nisbet 1967)150.

7. Soskice, *Metaphor*, 152 n. 206.

8. V. Lossky, *The Mystical Theology of the Eastern Church* (Cambridge: James Clarke, 1957), 25ff., analyzes the general Western tendency to see the relationship between cataphatic and apophatic theology in these terms, by reference to Thomas Aquinas, *Quaestiones Disputatae*, 7:5. He notes particularly the Thomist assertion that negations refer simply to the *modus significandi*—the mode according to which we understand finite perfections when we attribute them to God. In this Thomist view, from which Lossky dissents, it is still proper to affirm such perfections of God *modo sublimiori*, such affirmations relating to the *res significata*, in other words, to the perfection that is in God in a fashion other than the way it is in creatures.

9. Ibid., 33.

10. Ibid., 42–43.

11. See, for example, R. D. Williams, "The Philosophical Structures of Palamism," *Eastern Churches Review* 9 (1977): 27ff.; K. T. Ware, "The Debate about Palamism," *Eastern Churches Review* 9 (1977): 45ff..

12. See, for example, J. Pelikan, *Reformation of Church and Dogma (1300–1700)* (Chicago: University of Chicago Press, 1984), 187–203.

13. Soskice, *Metaphor*, 115ff.

14. F. Ferré, *Basic Modern Philosophy of Religion* (London: Allen and Unwin, 1968), 375.

15. M. Devitt and K. Sterelny, *Language and Reality: An Introduction to the Philosophy of Language* (Oxford: Basil Blackwell, 1987), 181.

16. R. Boyd, "Metaphor and Theory Change," in A. Ortony, ed., *Metaphor And Thought* (Cambridge: Cambridge University Press, 1979), 358.

17. Ibid., 358ff.

18. Such insights may, indeed, point to the way in which there is an arbitrary element in all attempts to "cut the world at its joints." From a scientific point of view, certainly, such questions arise from the holistic aspects

of modern physics, especially as interpreted by D. Bohm, *Wholeness and the Implicate Order* (London: Routledge & Kegan Paul, 1980). From a more purely philosophical point of view, too, there are important questions about "ontological relativity" posed by W. V. Quine in his *Ontological Relativity and Other Essays* (New York: Columbia University Press, 1969). It is not my purpose here, however, to explore the implications of such analyses to theology, other than simply to note their possible relevance to the paragraphs that follow.

19. J. Hick, *The Metaphor of God Incarnate* (London: SCM, 1992).

Chapter 11

1. K. Ward, *Religion and Revelation: A Theology of Revelation in the World's Religions* (Oxford: Clarendon, 1994), 343.

2. Rahner, "Visions," 144ff.

3. A third approach might also have been possible in terms of the work of John Macquarrie, who, while relying largely on the existentialist tradition in twentieth-century theology, goes beyond much of that tradition in the way he recognizes that saving historical events imply objective events. While he still believes, in an existentialist way, that we cannot and need not know the details or the actual content of such objective events—and in this respect his approach is one that is intrinsically different to that of this essay—the "phenomenological ontology" that he espouses could conceivably be expanded to develop something similar to my psychological-referential model, particularly in relation to the Easter experiences. For a good brief account of Macquarrie's position, see D. Jenkins, *The Scope and Limits of John Macquarrie's Existentialist Theology*, Studia Doctrinae Christianae 27 (Uppsala: Acta Universitatis Upsaliensia).

4. Attempts are sometimes made to define revelation in such a way as to exclude not only Eastern religions such as Buddhism, which does not employ the term revelation, but even those that do, such as Islam. Here I use revelation in the sense—consonant with the arguments of chap. 2—of that experience of salvation and new understanding that has been received subjectively as a gift rather than as the conclusion of a train of reasoning. This includes elements not only of all those religions that use the concept explicitly, but also those that use concepts such as "enlightenment."

5. See, for example, P. F. Knitter, *No Other Name?* (London: SCM, 1985), 145ff.

6. Hick's relativism—or, as he would prefer it, pluralism—does not, first of all, assert the equality of all religious traditions. In his article "On Grading Religions," in *Religious Studies* 17 (1981), for example, he states quite

clearly that, in relation to "the entire range of religious phenomena, no one is going to maintain that they are all on the same level of value or validity" (451). In his view, the proper criteria for comparison are, however, soteriological rather than referential: the only question that can properly be asked of a religious tradition is that of the degree of its success in bringing about "the transformation of human experience from self-centredness to Reality-centredness" (463). While this exclusively soteriological emphasis in Hick's understanding is interestingly expanded in relation to "truth claims" in chap. 20 of his *An Interpretation of Religion* (London: Macmillan, 1989), his denial that at least some questions about reference in theological language are in principle answerable fails, I would argue, to take into account those aspects of the nature of theological language explored in chaps. 6–10 of the present essay. Given the stage that both philosophical theology and interfaith dialogue have reached, on the other hand, it is certainly arguable that Hick's question is the only one that can be answered in practice at the present time, and that the view of interfaith dialogue that he propounds therefore represents a proper account of the criteria for its present phase. Until certain philosophical questions about reference and puzzle-solving ability have received clearer answers than are currently available, at any rate, it is certainly true that only tentative steps can be taken along the path of the essentially new phase of interfaith dialogue that I expound in the remainder of this chapter.

7. G. Lindbeck, *The Nature of Doctrine: Religion and Theology in a Postliberal Age* (Philadelphia: Westminster, 1984).

8. D. Stanesby, *Science, Religion and Reason* (London: Routledge, 1985) argues, for example, not only that a purely instrumentalist view of religious language "may well be a misconstruction of Wittgenstein" (178), but that it may also be incoherent insofar as Wittgenstein himself failed to see that religious beliefs and everyday or scientific ones may not be incommensurable. People like D. Z. Phillips, he says, are "doubtless correct in drawing our attention to the *expressive* nature of religious beliefs, but why should they not be literal and descriptive as well?" (179).

9. Clearly, conversion to an existing religious faith—the "revelation" to an individual of its authenticity—is extremely common in comparison with the occurrence of foundational revelatory experiences. This suggests that even if psychological factors are as important in the former as in the latter, they need not be as "finely tuned"—perhaps for reasons related to the sociology of religious communities. For example, while the revelation in the person of Jesus Christ could only have happened within the psycho-cultural niche provided by early first-century Judaism, that revelation

clearly had features (which in a Jungian framework would be described as "archetypal") that made it possible for its "truth" to be "revealed" in individual conversion experiences, not only to people within that culture but also to many who inhabited different niches.

10. R. Dawkins, *The Selfish Gene* (Oxford: Oxford University Press, 1967), 206.

11. Ibid., 207.

Afterword

1. R. Lull, *The Book of the Lover and the Beloved,* ed. Kenneth Leech (London: Sheldon, 1978), 110.

2. J. Polkinghorne, *Science and Christian Belief: Theological Reflections of a Bottom-Up Thinker* (London: SPCK, 1994), 1.

3. A. R. Peacocke, *Theology for a Scientific Age: Being and Becoming—Natural, Divine and Human,* enlarged ed. (London: SCM, 1993), x.

4. A. R. Peacocke, *God and the New Biology* (London: J. M. Dent & Sons, 1986), 128.

5. Ibid.

Index

miracles, 41
Moltmann, Jürgen , 16, 135 n.20
Monod, Jacques, 85
Montefiore, Hugh, 2
Moore, Aubrey, 13
Moore, J. R., 124 n.6
Murphey, 134 n.5
Murphey, Nancy, 50, 92
mysticism, 97, 99f.
mythmaking, as universal human
    practice, 40

natural processes, relation to
    sacraments, 18
natural theology, 3–6, 21, 81ff.
    neglect of divine revelation, 4,
    7, 44
    relation to positive theology, 6
naturalism, 63
Newton, Isaac, 86, 91
Newton-Smith, W. H., 134 n.8
nonfoundationalism, 91

O'Collins, G., 127 n.6

Pagels, Elaine, 134 n.13
panentheism, 18
pansacramental naturalism, 19f.,
    22, 30, 44, 54, 81, 107, 114
paradigm shift, 50, 85
patristic theology, insights into
    modern theology, 75, 81, 88,
    99f., 116
Peacocke, 135 n.1, 136 n.11
Peacocke, Arthur, xf., 3, 7–10,
    12f., 15–21, 30, 36f., 39, 57,
    82ff., 93, 117, 123 n.3, 135
    n.1, 136 n.11
Pelikan, J., 138 n.12
Perrin, Norman, 23
Phillips, D. Z., 130 n.12, 140 n.8
physics, relation to incarnation, 5
pluralistic theology, 108
Polkinghorne, John, x, 3f., 7ff.,

13–16, 82f., 117, 122, 123 n.3,
    125 n.3, 129 n.14
Popper, Karl, 50, 70
postfoundationalism, 57f., 72, 88f.
providence, doctrine of, 15ff.
psycho-cultural niche, 112ff.
psychological-referential model of
    revelatory experience, 66,
    107f., 109ff.
psychology
    challenge to theology, 84
    and religion, 24, 27–32, 35,
    40–44, 64f., 116
Putnam, Hilary, 93
puzzle-solving
    and the nature of Christian
    doctrine, 73ff., 78, 85, 89,
    101116
    in science and theology, 71ff.,
    116

Quine, W. V., 139 n.18

Rahner, Karl, 27–33, 65, 107
rationality, 60
realism, 91f., 96, 104f., 117
    and theological language, 96
    structural, 95, 98, 100f., 117
    substantial, 95, 98f.
reductionism, 36f., 41
reference, theory of, 93f., 97, 103f.
reference modes. *See* DC reference
    mode and IP reference mode
relativism, 110
religion, natural, 24ff., 43f.
religious experience
    non-christian , 33, 64
    psychological understanding,
    24, 27–32, 35f., 40–43
religious language
    apophatic nature, 99f.
    referential content, 108ff.
Resurrection, doctrine of, 22f.,
    31f., 65f., 73, 108f.

revelation, 21f., 35, 57, 60, 62, 64, 115f.
  in history, 45f.
  other faiths, 32
  special, 43f., 72, 82
revelatory experience, 63–66, 109
Roberts, L., 94
Robinson, J. M., 133 n.23
Russell, Bertrand, 48
Russell, D. S., 65

sacramental panentheism, 86f., 105
Sagovsky, N., 127 n.8
Schiavone, Christopher, 31
Schillebeeckx, Edward, 32
Schmemann, Alexander, 18
Schwartz, S. P., 137 n.12
science, rationality of, 50–53
scientist-apologists, 3, 84
Scope, 57
Sherry, P., 130 n.11
Soskice, Janet, 92, 97ff., 102, 104
soul (psyche), 35f., 42, 44
Stanesby, D., 140 n.8
Stoeger, William, 58
Swinburne, Richard, 41, 45, 51, 130 n.8

theologians, training in science, 2
theological anthropology, 83
theology and science, 77
  differences, 58f., 61
  experimentation, 60

theology
  autonomy from science, 8
  basis as a discipline, 38f.
  breakdown of traditional consensus, 77
  from the "top down", 76f., 89
  rationality of, 49, 52f.
theory autonomy, 37
Tindal, Matthew, 5
Tipler, F. J., 122 n.9
Torrance, 5–8, 21, 81ff., 136 n.3
Tyrrell, George, 24, 46, 128 n.10

unconscious, as a component of revelatory experience, 63
understanding, 59
Urs von Balthasar, Hans, 32

Vanstone, W. H., 16
visions, 27–32

Ward, Keith, 1, 22, 64f., 69f., 88, 107, 134 n.2, 135 n.16
Watts, Fraser, 14
Williams, R. D., 138 n.11
Wittgenstein, L., 46

Yannaras, C., 135 n.17

Zizioulas, John, 126 n.32, 135 n.18

CPSIA information can be obtained at www.ICGtesting.com
Printed in the USA
269355BV00004B/1/P

9 780800 632984